Urban and Van Eeden-Moorefield take the c[...]
methods and make it—dare I say—fun and [...]
stories and good humor, they demystify the research process and find ways to
connect research to everyday life and experiences. This book should be a
required supplementary text for every introductory research methods course.

—**William M. Trochim, PhD,** *Professor, Cornell University, Ithaca, NY*

The authors use vivid and engaging examples and masterfully crafted exhibits
to create an irresistible proposition to students: "You can do excellent research and enjoy doing it!" They creatively help readers understand and
make the choices involved in exemplary research. This book is an invaluable
asset for students in psychology and in the social and behavioral sciences
more generally.

—**Richard M. Lerner, PhD,** *Bergstrom Chair in Applied Developmental Science
and Director, Institute for Applied Research in Youth Development, Tufts University,
Medford, MA*

This book will help beginning researchers identify a meaningful and testable
research question as well as deal with basic choices in designing their study.
The accessible text and a host of tables guide readers through key issues in
designing and proposing a research project.

—**Melvin M. Mark, PhD,** *Professor and Head of Psychology, The Pennsylvania State
University, University Park*

Designing and
Proposing Your
Research Project

Concise Guides to Conducting Behavioral, Health, and Social Science Research Series

Designing and Proposing Your Research Project
Jennifer Brown Urban and Bradley Matheus van Eeden-Moorefield

Writing Your Psychology Research Paper
Scott A. Baldwin

Designing and Proposing Your Research Project

JENNIFER BROWN URBAN AND
BRADLEY MATHEUS VAN EEDEN-MOOREFIELD

**CONCISE GUIDES TO CONDUCTING BEHAVIORAL,
HEALTH, AND SOCIAL SCIENCE RESEARCH**

AMERICAN PSYCHOLOGICAL ASSOCIATION • *Washington, DC*

Published by
American Psychological Association
750 First Street, NE
Washington, DC 20002
www.apa.org

To order
APA Order Department
P.O. Box 92984
Washington, DC 20090-2984
Tel: (800) 374-2721; Direct: (202) 336-5510
Fax: (202) 336-5502; TDD/TTY: (202) 336-6123
Online: www.apa.org/pubs/books
E-mail: order@apa.org

In the U.K., Europe, Africa, and the Middle East, copies may be ordered from
American Psychological Association
3 Henrietta Street
Covent Garden, London
WC2E 8LU England

Typeset in Minion by Circle Graphics, Inc., Columbia, MD

Printer: Maple Press, York, PA
Cover Designer: Naylor Design, Washington, DC

The opinions and statements published are the responsibility of the authors, and such opinions and statements do not necessarily represent the policies of the American Psychological Association.

Library of Congress Cataloging-in-Publication Data
Names: Urban, Jennifer Brown, author. | van Eeden-Moorefield, Brad, author.
Title: Designing and proposing your research project / Jennifer Brown Urban
    and Bradley Matheus van Eeden-Moorefield.
Description: First edition. | Washington, DC : American Psychological
    Association, [2018] | Series: Concise guides to conducting behavioral and
    social science research | Includes bibliographical references and index.
Identifiers: LCCN 2017003496 | ISBN 9781433827082 | ISBN 1433827085
Subjects: LCSH: Psychology—Research—Methodology.
Classification: LCC BF76.5 .U73 2018 | DDC 150.72—dc23 LC record available at
https://lccn.loc.gov/2017003496

British Library Cataloguing-in-Publication Data
A CIP record is available from the British Library.

Printed in the United States of America
First Edition

http://dx.doi.org/10.1037/0000049-000

In loving memory of Sarah Kulkofsky. You were always a guiding light and helping hand. Your research methods course materials provided the initial starting point for my own enjoyment of teaching, and now writing, about research methods. Thank you.

—*Jennifer Brown Urban*

I dedicate this book to the many professors throughout my education and career who have inspired my passion for research methods.
To Dr. Natalie Oransky, you were my first introduction to research methods as an undergraduate and continue to be an inspiration.
To Dr. Betsy Lindsey, you pushed my critical eye and attention to detail during my master's program.
To Dr. Kay Pasley, you gave me space as a doctoral student to stretch my methodological passion and knowledge beyond what I thought possible.
To each of you, and the many others, thank you!

—*Bradley Matheus van Eeden-Moorefield*

Contents

Series Foreword

Why are you reading this book? Perhaps you have recently been assigned to write a research paper in an undergraduate course. Maybe you are considering graduate school in one of the behavioral, health, or social science disciplines, such as psychology, public health, nursing, or medicine, and know that having a strong research background gives you a major advantage in getting accepted. Maybe you simply want to know how to conduct research in these areas. Or perhaps you are interested in actually conducting your own study. Regardless of the reason, you are probably wondering—how do I start?

Conducting research can be analogous to cooking a meal for several people. Doing so involves planning (e.g., developing a menu), having adequate resources (e.g., having the correct pots, pans, carving knives, plates), knowing what the correct ingredients are (e.g., what spices are needed), properly cooking the meal (e.g., grilling vs. baking, knowing how long it takes to cook), adequately presenting the food (e.g., making the meal look appetizing), and so forth. Conducting research also involves planning, proper execution, having adequate resources, and presenting one's project in a meaningful manner. Both activities also involve creativity, persistence, caring, and ethical behavior. But just like cooking a meal for several people, conducting research should follow one of my favorite pieces of advice—"remember that the devil is in the details." If you want your dinner guests to find your meal tasty, you need to follow a recipe properly and measure the ingredients accurately (e.g., too much or little of some of the ingredients can make the entrée taste awful). Similarly, conducting research without properly paying attention to details can lead to erroneous results.

Okay, but what about your question—"How do I start?" This American Psychological Association (APA) book series provides detailed but user-friendly guides for conducting research in the behavioral, health, and social sciences from start to finish. I cannot help but think of another food analogy here—that is, the series will focus on everything from "soup to nuts." These short, practical books will guide the student/researcher through each stage of the process of developing, conducting, writing, and presenting a research project. Each book will focus on a single aspect of research, for example, choosing a research topic, following ethical guidelines when conducting research with humans, using appropriate statistical tools to analyze your data, and deciding which measures to use in your project. Each volume in this series will help you attend to the details of a specific activity. All volumes will help you complete important tasks and will include illustrative examples. Although the theory and conceptualization behind each activity are important to know, these books will focus especially on the "how to" of conducting research, so that you, the research student, can successfully carry out a meaningful research project.

This particular volume, by Jennifer Brown Urban and Bradley Matheus van Eeden-Moorefield, is required reading very early on. These authors focus on the earlier stages of the process—the careful planning, assembling of "ingredients," preparing, and proposing a research project. Thus, if you are ready to design your research project and need user-friendly guidelines, this book can be of immense aid.

So, the answer to the question "How do I start?" is simple: just turn the page and begin reading!

Best of luck!

—Arthur M. Nezu, PhD, DHL, ABPP
Series Editor

Designing and Proposing Your Research Project

1

Introduction

The first thing students typically feel when they learn they are required to take a research methods course for their major is dread. The very thought of research methods sends some students running to find another major. As professors, we appreciate the challenge of working with students who enter our classrooms less than excited about taking research methods. We love seeing their excitement and sense of accomplishment at the end of the semester after crafting their first research proposal. Is research methods challenging? Yes, absolutely. Is research methods fun? You might not think so right now, but we think it is, as do most of our former students.

We are confident we can convince you that it's certainly not as impossible as you may think. Our goal for this book is to help you get from Point A to Point Z. We break down the process of designing your research project into manageable steps and guide you through the decision-making process. Along the way, we also provide direction for writing up your research

http://dx.doi.org/10.1037/0000049-001
Designing and Proposing Your Research Project, by J. B. Urban and B. M. van Eeden-Moorefield
Copyright © 2018 by the American Psychological Association. All rights reserved.

proposal. By the end of this book, we hope you will feel a sense of accomplishment. The best way to learn about research is to get your hands dirty and actually experience what it's like to design your own research project. So, let's begin!

OUR STORY

Once upon a time, in a faraway land, we, the authors, were undergraduates taking our first research methods class. Now, you might be thinking, "Of course they liked taking research methods as undergrads; that's what they do now for a living!" Although this is true, we weren't born loving research; in fact, most people aren't born loving research. It's an acquired taste. For one of us (Jen), her undergraduate research methods course was actually pretty fun. Jen got to work with friends to develop a research project, collect data, write it up in a report, and present it to her classmates. She still remembers the research project to this day.

She and her friends were interested in whether people would follow directional signs that instructed people to do something that was contrary to what common sense would dictate. So they designed an observational study to test that research question. They went to the campus coffee shop and put a sign on the door that said "pull." It was one of those doors with a big bar across it that was obviously supposed to be pushed. Jen can't recall the study's findings, but she still remembers how much fun she had working on the project. It was this hands-on experience, as well as experience working in actual research labs as an undergrad, that ignited her love of social science research.

Brad took his first research class as a sophomore and remembers all the horror stories he heard from fellow psychology majors—"You will hate it; you will be bored out of your mind!"—and, of course, the untrue rumor "everyone fails their first time taking research methods." Certainly, there was no way that taking research was going to be as enjoyable as taking abnormal psychology and diagnosing everyone you know with every known disorder you read about and then some. He was soon proved wrong.

The first study Brad ever conducted was an observational study examining personal space. He worked as part of a research team and went to the library, where one team member went up to every 15th person who walked by the staircase and asked for the time. Team members varied how close they got to each person (1, 2, or 3 feet). A second and third team member recorded reactions. As you can predict, the closer they were, the more likely the random person was to back away (and sometimes not even respond). Brad admits that although this was a super fun study, there were times he felt a little awkward when he was a foot away from someone he did not know.

The second study lasted the entire semester and was a reexamination of the Wegner rebound effect—the classic white bear study. The basic premise is that telling someone they cannot think about something, like a white bear, makes them think about it more often than those who are told to think about white bears. How many of you will be thinking about white bears for the next hour? Don't do it! Amazingly, the results from Brad's study matched those of Dr. Wegner, who is known as the father of thought suppression research.

This experience of being able to find answers to questions using a systematic and reliable method (as opposed to WebMD or Wikipedia) was the coolest thing and ignited Brad's passion for research. Walking into the first research methods class, Brad was extremely anxious and did not know how he would survive. Fortunately, he had an incredible professor and fell in love with research.

So, how did we come to fall in love with research methods? Let's explain it using a dating analogy. The short answer is that we had some amazing "dates" with research methods that increased with frequency over time (i.e., we put in a lot of time and effort in and outside of class), and we did fun activities with research (i.e., designed and carried out two small studies), and we spent time communicating and getting to know about research methods (i.e., we read, thought, took notes, asked lots of questions, and listened for every detail). From this, a sincere passion for research methods developed that also resulted in a career for both of us.

Our unique undergraduate experiences helped us conceptualize this book. We want you to discover the joys of research for yourself, just as we did. This book will not sit in your bag all semester and be the book that you dread taking out to read. Our goal is that this book will be your guide, workbook, and manual and will help you develop a great research project and proposal. With that in mind, we approached each chapter with the goal of including less writing and more tables, figures, exhibits, and case studies to make the text as usable as possible.

ITERATIVE PROCESS, LINEAR TEXT

Putting research methods into a simple series of steps requires that we present this guide in a linear format. However, designing a research study is not a linear process. For example, sometimes it makes sense to think of your sampling plan before you map out your design plan. Sometimes it's better to figure out the design before the sample. Most of the time, it's an iterative process. As you make changes to one section, you will need to go back and rework earlier sections. This is especially true for those who conduct qualitative research.

One element should always come first, though, and that's determining your topic, research question, or hypothesis. These will guide all of the decisions you make as you design your study. Because this step is so critical, we cover it at the beginning of this book.

ASSUMPTIONS

In writing this book, we made several important assumptions.

First, we assume that this is not your only research methods book. We expect that this book will be used in conjunction with a research methods book that covers these topics in more detail.

Second, we assume that you are being asked to design your own research project. This book is intended as a guide to help you develop your own idea into a full research proposal. In fact, we have developed a companion website with additional helpful information, including an example outline of a research proposal (http://pubs.apa.org/books/supp/urban).

Third, we assume that you need to make a lot of choices and decisions in designing your study. This book is intended to help you make those choices. We will not provide a comprehensive overview of all possible research designs. Rather, we will present the most commonly used research designs, particularly those used by students.

Finally, it is important to understand that there is no such thing as a perfect study, or one that will provide all the answers to your questions. In fact, the best studies result in more questions than they do answers. Another way of stating this is that all studies have limitations: Your job is to become aware of some limitations and understand ways to improve on them in future research.

Many of you are likely feeling overwhelmed and wondering how you can learn everything about research, develop a research plan and proposal, submit an institutional review board application, carry out a study, analyze and write up the results, and everything else, all in one semester or maybe a year! Do you want the good or bad news first?

Let's get the bad out of the way: It takes a lot of work, period. The good news: Tens of thousands of students, and likely many more, have completed projects successfully under the same conditions for decades. Plus, you have this book to help you.

A NOTE ABOUT ETHICS AND READING LITERATURE

As you proceed with designing and proposing your own research project, one thing that is absolutely important to consider throughout the entire process is *ethics*—that is, how you will protect those who participate in your study from any harm or undue stress. Although a detailed discussion of ethics is beyond the scope of this book, we provide a quick overview of some of the main ethical considerations on the companion website (http://pubs.apa.org/books/supp/urban). To get you on the right path, we also created an ethics table that lists several tips and questions to ask yourself about the study you are planning. This table can be found on the companion website.

Similarly, throughout your research project you will no doubt find yourself reading many published studies to see what other work has been done. In our experience, when students read research studies, they often skip over the Method and Results sections. It is extremely tempting to do this because those sections often include a lot of unknown technical terminology, and many of us are taught to care only about the outcomes. However, if you carefully read the Method section of articles and use strategies similar to those listed, you can have greater confidence in designing and carrying out your own study. As an added bonus, this reading can provide you with citations to use when writing your Method section. We wish you luck and excitement as your begin the journey of designing your research project!

2

Choosing Your Research Question and Hypotheses

Choosing your research question and hypotheses is one of the most important steps in designing your research project. Your research question and hypotheses will guide every subsequent decision you make. One of the most common errors we see students make is to forget to lead with their question. Long before you can decide whether you will do a quantitative or qualitative study, or whether you will use a survey, an interview, or observational techniques, you must first determine your research question—that is, what you want to learn about your focal topic. It is your question that should determine every other decision about your project, and not the other way around. Take this conversation one of us had with a student as an example:

Student: I'm a quantitative researcher, so I'm going to be using a survey.

Professor: Well, what's your research question?

http://dx.doi.org/10.1037/0000049-002
Designing and Proposing Your Research Project, by J. B. Urban and B. M. van Eeden-Moorefield

Student: I'm not sure yet, but once I figure it out, I know that I'll be doing something quantitative.

Professor: [sighs and launches into a discussion of why this is a misguided approach].

Hopefully, you get the point that carefully choosing your research question and hypotheses is a critical first step in designing your research project. In this chapter, we help you identify and refine your research question.

RESEARCH QUESTIONS VERSUS HYPOTHESES

Before we get too far into a discussion of how to choose a research question and hypotheses, we want to clarify the distinction between research questions and hypotheses. A *hypothesis* is a clearly articulated statement about the expected relationship between a set of variables and is found only in quantitative studies. Also specific to quantitative studies, a *research question* is a clearly articulated question about a specific area of study that poses a suggested relationship between a set of variables. It may be easier to begin by developing a research question such as "Do standardized college admissions tests (e.g., SAT or ACT) predict academic success in college?" This can then be turned into a specific hypothesis, such as "High school GPA is a stronger predictor of academic success in college than SAT scores."

As in quantitative studies, qualitative research questions are central to planning a successful study. In fact, research questions are the most central feature of qualitative studies, whereas hypotheses are the most central guide for quantitative studies. However, there are a couple of key differences in the role of qualitative research questions. First, the research question you begin with might change several times during the research process such that the question you end up with looks fairly different from the question you began with. This is because an important part of the qualitative research process is to enter the field aware of your own potential biases, to be free of any strong preconceived ideas about potential findings (i.e., to have no hypothesis predicting what you expect to find), and to allow participants to guide you as they share their experiences. In other words, as the researcher, your responsibility is to tell the stories of your participants, not to confirm your ideas. Second, compared with quantitative research questions, qualitative research questions tend to be written more broadly, cannot be answered with yes or no (i.e., they are open-ended), and rely on a couple of subquestions to help specify the foci of a study.

Thus, the type of research question you develop will determine whether you should have a qualitative or quantitative study. The question determines the design, not the other way around. We discuss the distinctions between qualitative and quantitative studies later in this book, in Chapter 4.

WHERE DO SOCIAL RESEARCH QUESTIONS AND HYPOTHESES COME FROM?

The idea for, and the motivation behind, a research question or hypothesis can come from a number of places. Begin by thinking about and making a list of issues that you think have significance and potential for research. What is your passion? You can also browse through journals that seem interesting. Go to your library's reference page, and try clicking on the link for psychology-related journals (we're assuming your library web page organizes journals by discipline; if it doesn't, contact a reference librarian). Browse through the journal titles and see if any catch your eye. Then browse through the most recent table of contents for those journals. You can also try looking through the textbooks of classes that you found to be particularly interesting.

Faculty in your department are another great resource. Go to your department's web page and read up on what the professors in your program are researching. Better yet, set up an appointment and visit them to just chat about ideas. This happens so infrequently these days, and you would be surprised by how many faculty enjoy the opportunity to sit down face-to-face with students to talk. Some of them may even be looking for students to help them out with their research projects.

The best research questions are derived from a theory. Perhaps you read something in another course on a theory or topic that sounded interesting. What were you left wondering about after completing that reading? You may have noticed that in the Discussion section of most journal articles, the authors present future directions or a set of ideas for follow-up studies that would extend the reported findings or provide new, important information. This is an excellent source of ideas for your own research project.

Some people are motivated by the idea of solving real-world problems or coming up with policy solutions. These applied research questions may inform decision making or help with determining resource allocation. An example of an applied quantitative research question would be, "Is abstinence-only or comprehensive sex education more effective at preventing teen pregnancy?" whereas a qualitative study might ask, "What are the experiences of teens who received abstinence-only education and went on to become pregnant during adolescence?"

Alternatively, some researchers are motivated by the idea of advancing basic knowledge and adding to the body of knowledge on a particular topic. An example of a basic research question would be, "How do children's cognitive abilities affect memory retrieval?" A similar one from a qualitative grounded theory study (i.e., designed to develop a theory) might be, "What is the process by which children retrieve memories, and how does this process vary by age?"

Often researchers are motivated by their own personal observations or experiences. When faced with a student struggling to find a research topic, we pose the question "When you wake up in the morning and look outside your window or listen to music, what do you see or hear that really gets you going?" In other words, what are you passionate about? As we stated earlier, whatever topic you choose, it should be something that truly interests *you* (after all, you're the one who is going to have to live with the topic for at least a semester).

FINDING THE RIGHT FOCUS

Once you've decided on your general topic and developed an initial draft of your research question, the next step is making sure your question has the right focus. Some questions are so broad that it would take a lifetime to address the question, and some are so narrow that you could never get an adequate sample to effectively answer the question. We refer to this as the *Goldilocks problem*: Just as Goldilocks found one bowl of porridge to be much too hot and another to be much too cold, the same idea applies when figuring out the right focus for your research question. Goldilocks knew immediately when she had found that bowl of porridge that was just right. It might not be quite as obvious when looking for the just-right research question, but we hope the examples in Exhibit 2.1 will help you narrow in on the best research question for your project.

EVALUATING YOUR RESEARCH QUESTION

Once you have an idea of what your research question might be, you should evaluate it to make sure it is (a) feasible, (b) relevant, and (c) scientifically important. The first question you should ask yourself is whether you can actually design and carry out a study on your research question in the time that you have available for the project. Imagine that your research question asks whether college freshmen with high self-esteem are more likely to graduate from college. Your research design might logically be a longitudinal study in which you measure students' self-esteem when they are freshmen and follow them for several years to determine whether they graduate college. Although this is a great question and a good design, it is not feasible if you have only one semester (or even a year) to complete

Exhibit 2.1
Comparison of Wrong and Right Foci for a Research Question

Too broad:	What is the effect of divorce on kids?
Too narrow:	Does living with a single working mother in an urban environment after a parental divorce affect the math grades of 5-year-old girls?
Just right:	What is the effect of parental divorce on young children's academic achievement?
	How does parental divorce influence children's experiences with academic achievement?

your research project. An alternative, and somewhat related, question might be to ask whether college freshmen with high self-esteem are more likely to stay enrolled in college after freshman year or how college freshmen's perceptions of their own self-esteem influence their persistence. Make sure you carefully think through the logistics involved in answering your research question before you commit to it.

You should also ask yourself whether your question is socially relevant. Not all research questions will have a clear connection to societal needs. However, even the most basic research questions should be connected to broader social impacts. How does answering your research question benefit society? If you can't answer this, consider revising your research question. You should keep this realistic, though. We find that most students, and many faculty, tend to think their research will fix the world.

Finally, you need to make sure your research question is scientifically important. Just because a question is feasible and socially relevant doesn't mean it's scientifically important. Does your question advance knowledge? Has the question already been addressed? If it has been addressed, is there a need for a replication study? Check the research literature to get a sense of what we know, what we don't know, and what we need to find out next. This process will allow you to refine your idea (e.g., How many hours of studying does it take for college freshmen to earn at least a 3.0 GPA? How do supportive aunts and uncles help kids manage the stress of witnessing their parents divorce?).

In the process of collecting previous research to help with this task, students often have a difficult time finding research articles that best match their focus. Although collecting research is important at this stage, it also is an important step toward developing and writing a literature review during a later stage. Here are a few suggestions for finding relevant literature to get you started:

- Ask a reference librarian! They are amazing at pointing you in the right direction.
- Find good keywords.
- Start with a broad search in a library database (make sure to search only for peer-reviewed studies), and once you find a couple of articles

that match your topic, look at the terminology they used, and put those terms into a new search.

- Look for a recently published literature review on your topic.
- As you find articles that are a good fit for your topic, look at their reference list.
- As you find authors who have done research on your topic, do an author search on their name because they are likely to have published other articles on the same topic.
- Search within a journal that has provided several good articles.

If you can't find any recent publications on your topic, it may be there's a good reason. Perhaps the topic has been overexplored and researchers are no longer engaging in research on the topic. Perhaps your question is no longer appropriate given the state of knowledge in the field. For example, despite Freud's popular theory, given what we now know, it would no longer be appropriate to ask whether mothers are responsible for triggering schizophrenia in their children.

Now it's time to find a classmate or a friend you can talk with about your ideas. Explain to this person why you are interested in the topic. Then explain what makes the topic socially relevant. Finally, explain what makes the topic scientifically important. Did your classmate or friend buy your explanations? Did you? If not, then it's back to the drawing board. Exhibit 2.2 provides a partner exercise to help you with this.

APPLYING CONCEPTS
TO YOUR RESEARCH PROPOSAL

Now you're ready to write your research question paragraph, which explains why your research question is good. This paragraph will eventually make its way into your research proposal and will be connected to the purpose statement, which is covered in Chapter 3. Begin by explaining why the topic you selected is an important research topic. Note that you need to establish the importance of this topic to other people, not just yourself. Explain why this is a socially relevant and scientifically important question. Be sure to back up any statements about importance with

---

Exhibit 2.2

Obtaining Peer Review of Your Initial Research Question Paragraph and Justification

Find a partner, and trade what you each wrote for your initial research question paragraph and justification. You are now acting as peer reviewers. Peer review is an important part of the scientific process. As a reviewer, you must provide clear, detailed, and explicit feedback to the author. Use the questions below as a guide when developing your feedback. Make sure the author has adequately addressed each point. Be critical, and whenever possible, explicitly state whether the author has addressed or needs to address a point.

- What is the topic that will be researched? Is the topic clearly stated?
- Is the research question clearly stated? Does the question take the form of "What is the effect of _____ on _____?" Should the question be revised? How?
- Is the question too broad? Is it too narrow? What suggestions do you have for revisions to the question?
- Does the author convince you that the question is socially relevant? How?
- Does the author convince you that the question is scientifically important? How?
- Does the author back up statements about the importance of the topic with supporting facts? Are these facts appropriately cited?

---

supporting facts (e.g., statistics or citations from the published literature about the prevalence of the problem you are addressing or the size of the affected population).

Remember, your research question might state the relationship between two or more variables and should be specific enough that you could feasibly conduct an actual study. Many quantitative research questions take the form of "What is the effect of _____ on _____?" Many quantitative studies also include a hypothesis specifying the expected relationship between two or more variables. For example, "As _____ increases, _____ will also increase." Many qualitative research questions ask *what* or *how* and include a few different elements—for example, "What are the lived experiences (this term denotes use of a particular type of qualitative design, in this case phenomenological) of female freshman college students taking part in a living–learning program for future psychologists (population of interest) as they transition from living at home with a parent to living in a residence hall (further specification of the central phenomenon)?"

This introductory paragraph will be followed by a detailed literature review. At the end of the literature review, you will present (or restate) the purpose of the study and your own research question and hypotheses. Although we do not discuss how to do a literature review further in this book, we have included a few tips on the companion website (http://pubs.apa.org/books/supp/urban).

3

Choosing Your Study's Purpose

Now that you have a good sense of what is known (or not) about your topic (i.e., you have read a bunch of existing studies) and you have a good draft of your initial research question, it is time to select the best purpose for your study. Although the purpose is closely related to the research question, it is not the same thing. The research question (and hypotheses, if a study is quantitative) is used at the end of the purpose statement. This means you already have a piece of your statement completed.

At this point, it might be helpful to think of things in terms of a cone-shaped funnel. The Introduction starts broad (identify the problem, scope, a little about what we know, and the gap) and ends highly specific (the research question and/or hypothesis). The purpose statement is kind of like the middle of the funnel and connects the two ends—it is more specific than the larger problem under investigation but broader than the specific question and/or hypothesis. As you will see, instead of identifying

http://dx.doi.org/10.1037/0000049-003
Designing and Proposing Your Research Project, by J. B. Urban and B. M. van Eeden-Moorefield

only what question you will answer, the purpose statement is where you begin sharing some details about the population you will study, the design of your study, the theory you plan to use, and so forth. Importantly, you want your purpose type to match your research question.

TYPES OF RESEARCH PURPOSES

Table 3.1 identifies the three main types of research purpose: exploratory, descriptive, and explanatory (there are others, such as evaluation); the table also lists considerations for selecting the best overall purpose to fit your study and an example purpose statement for each type. Importantly,

Table 3.1

Types of Purpose Statements and Tips for Selecting the Right One for You

Type	Key considerations for selecting	Example purpose statement
Exploratory	Ideal when a research topic, phenomenon, or concept is new and little is known about it	The purpose of this study is to conduct interviews with high school juniors who plan to go to college to explore how this group uses social media to select colleges to which they want to apply.
Descriptive	Ideal when we know a little about a newer concept but not enough to be able to describe it or how it relates to other concepts	The aim of the current study is to understand how first-semester college freshmen at a southern historically Black college or university (HBCU) describe their lived experiences as they transition from attending primarily White high schools to attending an HBCU.
Explanatory	Ideal when we have a strong understanding of how concepts relate to one another but wish to explain the nature of the relationships more strongly (e.g., whether concepts precede or predict another or are simply related to each other)	The current study's purpose is to explain which high school performance indicators (GPA, number of advanced placement courses taken) and community involvement indicators (hours of community service provided in the past 3 months, number of volunteer organizations participated in) best predict success among a random sample of freshman college students at the end of their 1st year.

these purposes can be used for quantitative, qualitative, or mixed-methods studies, and sometimes one study has more than one purpose.

Let's start with a simple example. Currently, scientists are exploring space looking for the existence of life beyond Earth. We know there is a habitable zone around most suns that has a high likelihood of providing many of the necessary ingredients to support life. Scientists are conducting *exploratory studies* to evaluate these areas and the planets in them for any signs that life might exist.

Let's pretend the scientists find life. The next step would be to conduct *descriptive studies* that have a goal of describing (a) the conditions and characteristics of that planet such that it would be easier to identify planets in other parts of the galaxy likely to have life; or (b) more interesting, the alien species, including what they look like, what materials they use, whether there are signs of weapons on the planet, and whether the aliens have the means to communicate with or visit us on Earth.

Once we know this information, scientists could conduct *explanatory studies* to predict whether other planets have life or whether the aliens are likely friendly or hostile. The main takeaway here is that the amount of information that exists about a phenomenon will guide which research purpose is best for your study.

APPLYING CONCEPTS TO YOUR RESEARCH PROPOSAL

Once you have a purpose, it is time to write it up. Purpose statements typically are placed at the end of the Introduction. When we were in school, we received a lot of comments from professors about how our papers lacked flow and logic. At the time, we had no clue what they meant. But there is a natural flow and logic to the ideas of any story, and the Introduction is part of the research story, with the purpose statement acting as both a summary of the Introduction and a foreshadowing of the rest of the research proposal. As a quick review, the elements of an Introduction (in order) include what the "problem" is, how big the problem is (i.e., the scope), what makes it important and significant (sometimes referred to as the *"so what?"* of a study), what you know in broad overview, what you don't know (i.e., the gap your study seeks to fill), and finally the purpose statement. Exhibit 3.1 provides more general writing tips to consider.

The purpose statement contains several elements, listed below. As you will notice, some elements of the purpose statement need to be added in later as you work through the rest of the text of your proposal (remember, we said that designing and proposing a research project is an iterative process). For now, take a guess at these six elements of your purpose statement:

1. A phrase that tells the reader, "This is the purpose statement" (e.g., "The purpose of this study is . . . ," "The aim of this study is . . .").
2. The type of purpose—exploratory, descriptive, or explanatory. There are several synonyms for these words; however, we suggest using one of these three until you have more practice.

Exhibit 3.1

Tips for Scientific Writing

- Avoid using direct quotations. In scientific writing, avoid quoting unless it is truly necessary. Instead, paraphrase and cite your source.
- Avoid using strong language such as "It is *proven* that low-resource neighborhoods *cause* bad academic achievement." Things are rarely *proven*; there is always room for some doubt. Causal language can only be used when a true experiment is conducted (we discuss more about this in Chapter 6).
- Avoid using contractions (e.g., don't, can't, won't) or colloquial phrases (e.g., "on the other hand") in formal academic papers. It's OK in less-formal writing, such as in this book.
- In-text citations should include the authors' last names and the year of publication (e.g., Smith & Jones, 2015), not the title of the article or where the research was conducted.
- When you cite a source, be sure to provide enough information in the reference list so that the reader can go out and find the exact document you are citing.

3. The topic and population being studied.
4. The theoretical framework being used.
5. Words (i.e., terminology) that provide the reader with a strong indication of the design used. We will address terminology throughout the chapters ahead.
6. Draft research questions and (if applicable) hypotheses. These are listed at the end of the purpose statement.

The fifth element—terminology—is important, and we will return to it several times in this book. All sections of a research study and manuscript are connected and must be cohesive. Each type of research has its own terminology that is difficult even for the most skilled researcher to get correct all of the time. The point is that word choice matters. Two simple examples will get you thinking.

First, suppose a researcher states that the purpose of her study is to explain the *causal relationship* between time spent on Facebook and GPA. The use of the word *causal* tells the reader that some type of experimental design will be used for the study. If the reader gets to the Method section and reads that a case study will be conducted, this would be a problematic inconsistency.

Second, if a study used a phenomenological approach, the purpose statement should include words like *understand* and *lived experience* because these are central purposes of any phenomenological study. Take a look at the example purpose statements in Table 3.1, and see whether you can identify each of the elements listed above.

4

Choosing Whether to Use a Qualitative, Quantitative, or Mixed-Methods Approach

By now you have a topic for your research project, a working research question and hypothesis, and a draft purpose statement. Now it's time to decide which approach—qualitative, quantitative, or mixed methods—is the best fit for your project. Although we realize that you might have decided on an approach before getting to this point, remember that we believe it is important to let your research question determine the approach and methods, so that you can answer the question you have in mind, rather than altering the question to fit the approach. In other words, we encourage you to have a variety of approaches and methods available in your tool kit so that you are not limited in the topics you can study and questions you can ask. Also remember that we view research as an iterative process, so you will want to continuously refine the wording for your research question, hypothesis, and purpose statement.

http://dx.doi.org/10.1037/0000049-004
Designing and Proposing Your Research Project, by J. B. Urban and B. M. van Eeden-Moorefield

To help you decide on your research approach, this chapter focuses on identifying the similarities and differences between primarily qualitative and quantitative approaches. However, we also provide a glimpse into various mixed-methods approaches that combine qualitative and quantitative methods within a single study, and this material can be found on the companion website (http://pubs.apa.org/books/supp/urban).

QUALITATIVE VERSUS QUANTITATIVE APPROACHES

In the most basic sense, *qualitative* approaches deal with people's actual words, life stories, pictures, videos, and so forth. For example, we could ask a group of you to tell us the story of how you settled into your first semester at college and made new friends. We could then sort through your stories to identify common patterns, such as joining organizations, going to class, or meeting people in the student center when you skipped class (but none of us ever did that, right?). These are forms of qualitative data.

Alternatively, *quantitative* approaches deal with numbers (e.g., rankings on a scale, GPA, weight). Using the previous example, maybe we asked you to identify how likely you were to make new friends in certain places and provided you a list of several place options. In this scenario, we might learn that you met most of your new friends at the student center, but we likely would have missed out on the part of your story that told us why you were at the student center meeting new people (e.g., because you skipped class).

All of the information gathered using both qualitative and quantitative approaches is important; it simply is different because we used different approaches. Table 4.1 lists several more characteristics that help distinguish qualitative and quantitative approaches and provides a way for you to think about your topic and what type of research approach you want to use. For each characteristic, read the two options in the table, and place an *X* next to the option you think best fits your project. In doing so, you might find that the majority, or even all, of your *X*s end up in one column or the other. If you end up with *X*s in both columns, a mixed-methods study might be best for you. We caution newer researchers about attempting mixed-methods studies, however, because they usually are

Table 4.1

Checklist for Evaluating Whether Your Study Should Use a Qualitative or Quantitative Approach

General characteristics of your study	X	Your study is likely qualitative if . . .	X	Your study is likely quantitative if . . .
Nature of reality and truth (ontology)		There are many realities and truths waiting to be discovered (i.e., there are many answers), and they constantly change.		There is one truth and reality, and it can be discovered (i.e., there is only one correct answer).
Bias and values		Bias and values of researchers exist, and we simply should be up front about them (e.g., use of reflexivity). Researchers are subjective.		Bias and values of researchers are not present because the methods they use control for it. Researchers are objective.
Role of the researcher		A high level of interaction with participants is planned. For example, you might collect data by interviewing all participants for 2 hours each.		A low level of interaction with participants is planned. For example, you might post a survey online and never interact with participants.
How you arrive at answers		An inductive process is used; findings emerge over the course of the study.		A deductive process is used; expected results are stated before data collection begins through use of specific hypotheses.

(continues)

Table 4.1

Checklist for Evaluating Whether Your Study Should Use a Qualitative or Quantitative Approach (*Continued*)

General characteristics of your study	X	Your study is likely qualitative if . . .	X	Your study is likely quantitative if . . .
Design elements		An open and flexible, inductive process is planned. For example, you can alter interview questions and the topic during data collection because several participants helped you realize you were asking the wrong questions.		A more controlled (e.g., laboratory setting), deductive process is planned. For example, you can control the time of day a survey is given, and everyone is given the exact same questions and directions.
Data collection process		The process can adapt and emerge over the course of the study. The researcher follows the participants.		The process is set before data collection begins and cannot change. The researcher leads the participants.
Purpose of data		Data provide depth of understanding and focus on uncovering meaning, experience, discourse, and so forth; participant quotes are used.		Data are quantifiable and can be reduced to numbers.
Reach		A narrow and contextual understanding specific only to the sample in your study is a goal.		Generalizability to many, or all, people is a goal.

Table 4.1				
Checklist for Evaluating Whether Your Study Should Use a Qualitative or Quantitative Approach (*Continued*)				
General characteristics of your study	X	Your study is likely qualitative if . . .	X	Your study is likely quantitative if . . .
Data quality		In-depth information is contained in participant quotes and sought through the quality of interview questions and prompts asked.		Measures and scales that demonstrate reliability and validity are used.
Analysis		You enjoy finding patterns in words, pictures, music, stories, and so forth.		You enjoy playing with numbers.

more difficult and involve more time. So you might want simply to see which column has the most Xs and use that approach for your project.

APPLYING CONCEPTS TO YOUR RESEARCH PROPOSAL

We hope that you now have a little better sense of the best approach for your project. So, it's time to take an even more specific look at the differences between qualitative and quantitative studies. We developed Table 4.2 to help with this. You will notice two main columns, one for qualitative and one for quantitative. Each column is divided into several cells that represent all the main parts of a research proposal and a journal article. We believe Table 4.2 will be helpful in three ways.

First, you can compare information about each part of a qualitative or quantitative proposal or journal article. This will help you see some of the main similarities and differences, and it also will help you see some of the many different methodological options you have for each approach.

Table 4.2

Anatomy of a Research Article and Comparison of Qualitative and Quantitative Approaches to Research

Section	Qualitative approach	Quantitative approach
	Introduction and literature review	
Research problem and scope	Main topic or problem being studied and how widespread or how much of a problem it is.	
Importance or significance	*"So what?"* question: Why your topic is important and what potential contribution studying it could make.	
Conceptual framework or theory	General background of the framework or theory and its assumptions, connection to your research question, and what it suggests about your topic. The framework or theory should be consistent with typical epistemologies used in qualitative studies, in which there are multiple realities and truths that change across time and context, many of which are influenced by power relations in society.	General background of the theory and its assumptions and relevant variables, discussion of what the framework or theory would say about your topic, and demonstration of how it relates to the hypothesis you proposed. The framework or theory should be consistent with typical epistemologies used in quantitative studies, in which there is one reality and one truth that can be known and research is used to know it.
Previous research	Review of previous studies, including reference to the samples and methods used across studies and, ideally, a critical and integrated review	
Gap in the literature	General overview of what is known about a topic, followed by a statement of what is *not* known and why this matters, leading to the purpose statement showing how you plan to fill the gap	
Purpose statement	Goals or aims and general description of your study	

Table 4.2

Anatomy of a Research Article and Comparison of Qualitative and Quantitative Approaches to Research (*Continued*)

Section	Qualitative approach	Quantitative approach
Research question	Research question detailing the central focus of the study and what you want to learn about it. When worded correctly, the research question indicates the design and methods of the study, theoretical framework, and population of interest but does not predict a particular set of findings. Subquestions may be used to further define the focus of a main research question.	Basic research question and hypotheses making specific predictions about what you expect the results of your study to be. When worded correctly, the research question and hypotheses indicate the level of measurement for each variable, the type of statistical test that will be used, and sometimes the study design.
Method		
Design	Action research, autoethnography, biography, case study, discourse analysis, ethnography, ethnomethodology, general qualitative design, grounded theory, hermeneutics, naturalism, participatory action, phenomenology, photovoice, symbolic interaction	Nonequivalent groups, one-shot case study, posttest only, regression discontinuity, single subject, static group comparison, time series, true experiment (pretest–posttest or Solomon)
Subdesign	Cross-sectional, longitudinal	
Sample type	Convenience, purposive, quota, snowball	Cluster, convenience, multistage probability, simple random, snowball, stratified random, systematic random, time–space
Sample description	Size and how determined (e.g., data saturation), inclusion and exclusion criteria, demographics (e.g., ethnicity, gender, race, sexual orientation, socioeconomic status)	Size and how determined, inclusion and exclusion criteria, demographics (e.g., ethnicity, gender, race, sexual orientation, socioeconomic status)

(continues)

31

Table 4.2

Anatomy of a Research Article and Comparison of Qualitative and Quantitative Approaches to Research (*Continued*)

Section	Qualitative approach	Quantitative approach
Sampling strategies	Recruitment procedures	
Data collection method	Content analysis, focus group, in-depth interview, written texts, photovoice, observation, secondary data	Survey, observation, secondary data, interview
Collection medium	In-person, telephone, virtual	In-person, computer-mediated, mail, telephone, virtual
Data collection procedures	How rapport is established and how people participate throughout each part of the study; includes informed consent and other ethical practices	How people participate throughout each part of the study; includes informed consent and other ethical practices such as debriefing
Data collection techniques	Questions, content coding scheme: structured, semistructured, unstructured formats; interview questions and example probing questions; specific coding scheme developed for use or that emerges during coding	Measurement (variables and scales): independent, dependent, mediator, moderator, control, descriptive; names of existing scales used, if any; scoring methods; response options; range and meaning of scores
Quality of data	Trustworthiness: credibility; dependability; negative case analysis; plausibility; reflexivity; thick, rich description; transferability; triangulation	Evidence of validity, reliability, and fairness: empirical and procedure validity indicators (e.g., internal structure, test content, response processes, relations to other measures); Cronbach's alpha, measurement error; evidence of fairness in testing and test development
Data analysis	Constant comparative analysis, discourse analysis, grounded theory analysis, thematic analysis or interpretive analysis	Analysis of variance, chi square, correlation, factor analysis, hierarchical linear modeling, multivariate analysis of variance, path analysis, regression (logistic, multiple, simple), structural equation modeling, t test

Table 4.2		
Anatomy of a Research Article and Comparison of Qualitative and Quantitative Approaches to Research (*Continued*)		
Section	Qualitative approach	Quantitative approach
	Findings or Results and Discussion	
Findings or results	Theme 1 (subthemes):	Hypothesis 1:
	Theme 2+ (subthemes):	Hypothesis 2+:
Takeaway point of results and discussion		
Future research needs		
	Overall article	
Strengths		
Weaknesses		
Notes		

Note. To use this table to summarize articles, type the reference citation at the top of each summary, and don't forget the digital object identifier so you can easily access the article again.

For example, you will notice that both approaches require you to identify a gap in the literature. However, you will also notice that qualitative studies use research questions, whereas quantitative studies rely mainly on hypotheses. We realize this can be a little confusing because, technically, all studies need a basic research question as a starting point, and it might be easier to consider this as the topic or problem being studied. However, the most central part of a quantitative study is its hypothesis, and for a qualitative study it is its specific, well-developed research question.

Second, as you design your study, we suggest using a blank version of this table and fill in the cells with information about your project plans. This can be a great way to gather your ideas and make sure they fit with your selected approach, and then you can write your research proposal from the completed table. It might also provide a good way to get feedback from your instructor.

Finally, you can use a blank copy of the table as a way to guide your note taking when you read research articles. We even included cells where you can record the findings or results, strengths, and weaknesses. Often when students begin reading research, they are not sure what information to take away from the articles (i.e., what is important), so they end up highlighting almost every sentence. Each cell represents the most critical and useful information from an article and includes the buzzwords to look for as you read. Using this table does require a little bit more work on your part on the front end, but it will save you a lot of time later in the process.

5

Understanding Terms for Quantitative Studies: Concepts, Constructs, and Variables

When you started thinking about your research question or hypothesis, the first thing you probably did was to think about what concepts or constructs were of particular interest to you. Then, you probably thought about how they were related to one another. You may have hypothesized that one had a positive (or negative) effect on another. Without even realizing it, you may have identified the variables for a quantitative study (the focus of this chapter). Now you're ready to think about your design and measurement plan. Let's take it back a few steps and begin with a few definitions.

DEFINING AND DISTINGUISHING CONCEPTS, CONSTRUCTS, AND VARIABLES

A *concept* is a label we apply to things that share similar characteristics. In other words, they're things we think belong in the same category. Take a look at the images in Figure 5.1. You probably recognize something like

http://dx.doi.org/10.1037/0000049-005
Designing and Proposing Your Research Project, by J. B. Urban and B. M. van Eeden-Moorefield

Figure 5.1

Identifying concepts: Which image doesn't belong?

this from your workbooks as a kid when you were asked to circle the item that doesn't belong. When you did this, you were identifying a concept (in this case, farm animals). Not too difficult, right?

Now here's where it gets a little more complicated. Concepts are things that are tangible or can be pictured easily. *Constructs*, on the other hand, are things that exist but cannot be directly observed. Constructs include things like happiness, depression, sexism, and self-esteem. These all exist, but you can't actually see or touch them. Think about it: Could you create something like what is pictured in Figure 5.1 for self-esteem? Nope. In order to observe constructs, you have to use a measure. For example, to observe and measure sexism, you would need to come up with a list of characteristics or observable behaviors that would let you measure whether sexism exists. Your list might include things such as paying women less than men for the same work, using demeaning terms to describe women, providing more opportunities for promotion to men, telling sexist jokes, and the like. You could then turn this list into a survey measure.

Earlier, we mentioned that when you started thinking about your research question or hypothesis, the first thing you probably did was to think about the concepts and constructs that are most interesting to you. In the context of a research project, these concepts and constructs are called *variables*. Variables have two key qualities. First, a variable is something that is thought to influence something or be influenced by something. Second, a variable has at least two possible values.

Let's start with the first key quality. Imagine that we were to say that hair color is thought to influence choice of college major. Our assertion makes reference to two variables and their relationship: (a) hair color and (b) choice of college major. Hair color is a variable because it is thought to influence choice of college major. Choice of college major is a variable because it is thought to be influenced by hair color. Exhibit 5.1 provides a list of statements. See if you can identify the variables in each statement.

Now on to the second key quality: A variable has at least two possible values. Take, for example, the variable gender. It has at least three possible values: male, female, and transgender. The variable marital status has five possible values: never married, married, legally separated, divorced, and widowed. The number of possible values for a particular variable may vary depending upon your topic and sample. We will return to this idea and explain it with more detail in Chapter 8.

Now that you've got the idea of variables down, it's time to make it a little more complicated. Often variables are influenced by more than one thing. For example, choice of major might be influenced by GPA, self-esteem, and gender. College graduation rates might be influenced by major, GPA, living on campus, and involvement in social activities. See Exhibit 5.2 for some practice identifying variables and listing attributes.

Exhibit 5.1

Identify the Variables in Each Statement

1. GPA is thought to influence the likelihood of graduation.
2. Average amount of sleep each night is thought to be influenced by employment status.
3. Participation in Greek life is thought to influence drinking behavior.
4. Social media use is thought to influence popularity.
5. Style of dress is thought to be influenced by music preference.

Answers: 1. GPA and likelihood of graduation; 2. average amount of sleep, employment status; 3. participation in Greek life, drinking behavior; 4. social media use, popularity; 5. style of dress, music preference.

Exhibit 5.2

Identify the Variables in Each Statement and the Characteristics or Attributes of Each Variable

1. Political affiliation is influenced by gender and race.

2. Living on campus is influenced by geographic distance from campus to home and attachment to parents.

Answers: 1. political affiliation (Democrat, Republican, Independent, other), gender (male, female, other), race (White, Black, Asian, Hispanic, mixed, other); 2. living on campus (live on campus, live off campus), geographic distance from campus to home (less than 30 miles, 31 miles to 60 miles, 61 miles to 90 miles, 91 miles or more), attachment to parents (not attached at all, somewhat attached, very attached).

IDENTIFYING VARIABLES IN HYPOTHESES

You can now confidently identify variables, but what you're really interested in is testing the relationship between variables. Once you have identified the variables you are most interested in studying, the next step is to suggest a relationship between the variables. A *hypothesis* is a suggested relationship between two or more variables that is testable. Keep in mind that when you construct a hypothesis, you are not stating that it is actually true. Rather, you construct the hypothesis in order to test whether or not it is supported statistically. Hypotheses can be stated in a general way: Time spent studying affects GPA. They can also be stated in a more specific way, which is preferable: The more time students spend studying, the higher their GPA will be. Sometimes it is easy to identify the variables in a hypothesis, but other times it is a bit trickier. Read the hypotheses in Exhibit 5.3 and see if you can identify the variables.

Independent and Dependent Variables

Let's imagine that we have identified two variables that interest us: gender and college major. Which of the following statements makes more sense?

Exhibit 5.3

Identify the Variables in Each Hypothesis

1. Men are more likely than women to major in engineering.
2. Students who drink alcohol more than twice a week are more likely to earn lower grades than students who drink less.
3. Students who commute to school are less likely to feel a sense of belonging to school than students who live on campus.

Answers: 1. gender, college major; 2. drinking behavior, grades; 3. living arrangement, sense of belonging.

- A person's gender influences which college major they pursue.
- A person's college major influences their gender.

It's pretty clear that only the first statement makes sense. When a variable influences another variable, it's the "cause" variable, or *independent* variable. When a variable is influenced by another variable, it's the "effect" variable, or *dependent* variable. Keep in mind that whether a variable is independent or dependent has to do with how it is phrased in the hypothesis. Exhibit 5.4 reviews the hypotheses you just read. See if you can identify the independent and dependent variables.

Exhibit 5.4

Identify the Independent Variables and Dependent Variables in Each Hypothesis

1. Men are more likely than women to major in engineering.
2. Students who drink alcohol more than twice a week are more likely to earn lower grades than students who drink less.
3. Students who commute to school are less likely to feel a sense of belonging to school than students who live on campus.

Answers: 1. gender (independent), college major (dependent); 2. drinking behavior (independent), grades (dependent); 3. living arrangement (independent), sense of belonging (dependent).

Control and Extraneous Variables

In addition to independent and dependent variables, we sometimes identify additional variables that are not the key variables we are interested in but that we think might somehow influence our variables of interest. Imagine, for example, that our hypothesis is that high school GPA predicts graduation from college. Although we might find a relationship between high school GPA and college graduation rates, it could be due to an extraneous third variable— for example, parental income (see Figure 5.2). We would want to include a measure of parental income so that we could test whether the relationship between high school GPA and college graduation rates is actually explained by parental income. In this example, parental income is the control variable.

Using control variables allows us to test whether a relationship exists between the independent variable (GPA) and the dependent variable (college graduation) while holding the control variable (parental income) constant. In many studies, demographic variables (e.g., gender, race, income, marital status) are used as control variables.

Positive and Negative Relationships

The relationship between two variables can be either positive or negative. The terms *positive* and *negative* are not used to mean good or bad. In the

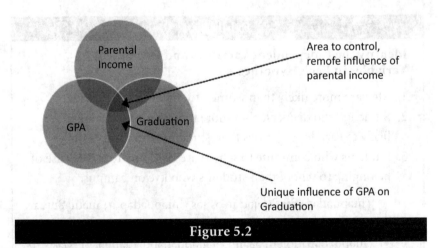

Figure 5.2

In this example, parental income is the extraneous and control variable.

context of variables, *positive* means the same and *negative* means different. In a positive relationship, the variables vary in the same direction. In a negative relationship, the variables vary in a different or the opposite direction.

In the hypothesis "Increased studying causes better grades," the relationship between studying and grades is positive because the two variables vary in the same direction. The more you study (an increase), the better your grades get (another increase). In the hypothesis "Increased studying causes fewer hangovers," the relationship between studying and hangovers is negative because the two variables vary in the opposite direction. The more you study (an increase), the fewer hangovers you get (a decrease). In positive relationships, both variables increase (increase in the independent variable and increase in the dependent variable), or both variables decrease (decrease in the independent variable and decrease in the dependent variable). In negative relationships, one variable increases and the other decreases (increase in the independent variable and decrease in the dependent variable, or decrease in the independent variable and increase in the dependent variable).

CASE STUDY: DR. GILMORE, PART 1

The case study in Exhibit 5.5 brings all of this together. Read it and answer the questions. Review your answers with a colleague.

APPLYING CONCEPTS TO YOUR RESEARCH PROPOSAL

Now it's time to apply what you've learned in this chapter to your own study. Reread your research question. What are the independent and dependent variables? If this is unclear, rewrite the research question to clarify. Then reread your hypothesis. What is the expected direction of association between the variables?

Exhibit 5.5

Case Study of Dr. Gilmore, Part 1

Dr. Gilmore has volunteered at several youth-serving organizations in her community, such as the YMCA and Girl Scouts, for the past few years. She has noticed that the youth who participate in the extracurricular programs offered by these organizations seem to be less likely to engage in risky behaviors such as drinking or smoking than their peers who engage in limited or no extracurricular activities. She is interested in conducting a formal study to explore whether or not extracurricular activity participation is related to risk-taking behavior. Dr. Gilmore hypothesizes that youth who spend more time in extracurricular activities will exhibit lower levels of risk-taking behaviors than youth who spend little to no time in extracurricular activities.

1. What are the variables in Dr. Gilmore's study?
2. What are the characteristics or attributes of the variables in Dr. Gilmore's study?
3. What is the independent variable?
4. What is the dependent variable?
5. Does Dr. Gilmore think that the relationship between the variables is positive or negative? Explain.

Answers: 1. extracurricular activity participation, risk-taking behavior; 2. extracurricular activity participation (high, medium, low; participation, no participation), risk-taking behavior (high, medium, low, none); 3. extracurricular activity participation; 4. risk-taking behavior; 5. negative—as activity participation goes up, risk-taking behavior goes down.

6

Choosing Your Design

Now you are ready to think about and select the design for your research study. There are several important things to consider, the most important being what you hope to accomplish with your study. The kinds of claims you are able to make depend largely on the type of design you choose. Is your goal to establish a causal relationship between two or more variables? Is your goal to gain a deeper understanding of a relatively underexplored topic? Is your goal to understand developmental processes? Are you conducting your study in a controlled laboratory setting or out in the real world? Your answers to these questions will help determine the best design to use.

In this chapter, we describe several of the most commonly used designs. Before we do that, it's important to understand the distinction between correlation and causation and what is needed to establish a causal relationship when that is a goal of your study.

---

http://dx.doi.org/10.1037/0000049-006
Designing and Proposing Your Research Project, by J. B. Urban and B. M. van Eeden-Moorefield

CORRELATION VERSUS CAUSATION

You may have heard the phrase "correlation does not equal causation" before, but what does it mean? *Correlation* means that changes in one variable are associated with changes in another. For example, sales of snow boots and sales of hot chocolate are correlated (both increase in the winter and decrease in the summer). The problem is, just because we have evidence that two variables are correlated doesn't mean that one causes the other. You wouldn't conclude that sales of snow boots cause sales of hot chocolate or that sales of hot chocolate cause sales of snow boots. In other words, we don't know which variable causes which or whether there is a third, causal variable (in this case, winter).

ESTABLISHING CAUSAL RELATIONSHIPS

In order to establish that there is a cause–effect relationship between variables, three criteria must be met: (a) temporal precedence; (b) covariation of cause and effect; and (c) no plausible alternative explanations. Imagine that we wanted to conduct a study, and our hypothesis is that taking advanced placement classes in high school causes higher scores on standardized tests. The first thing we need to do is demonstrate that the cause (in this case, taking advanced placement classes in high school) happens before the effect (higher scores on standardized tests): This is what is called establishing *temporal precedence*. The second thing we need to demonstrate is that there is a relationship between the independent variable (the cause) and the dependent variable (the effect). In our example, we have to demonstrate both that students who take advanced placement classes in high school have higher scores on standardized tests and that students who don't take advanced placement classes in high school have lower scores on standardized tests: This is what is called establishing *covariation of cause and effect*. Finally, we have to demonstrate that no other variable could possibly be responsible for the effect. For example, students who take more advanced placement classes in high school might have better study habits than students who don't take advanced placement classes in high school. Thus, the higher scores on standardized tests have a *plausible alternative explanation*: better study habits.

Some research designs are better than others at addressing these three criteria for establishing a causal relationship. In the following sections, we discuss some of the most commonly used research designs.

TRUE EXPERIMENTS

True experiments, which use random assignment to groups, are the most effective design for addressing the three criteria for establishing a causal relationship. They are also a good design to consider if the purpose of your study is explanatory. These designs do the best job of establishing internal validity (see Chapter 9).

True experiments are particularly good at meeting the criteria of no plausible alternative explanation and covariation of cause and effect by using random assignment to groups. In order to address these criteria, you need to have two groups that are equivalent at the beginning of your study. The only thing that will differ between them is that one group will get the independent variable and the other group will not. Randomly assigning your participants to groups ensures that the two groups are the same. *Random assignment* means that you put study participants into either a treatment group (that gets the independent variable) or a control group (that doesn't get the independent variable) based on chance. Think about our example: If we took a bunch of high school kids and randomly assigned some of them to advanced placement classes and others to regular classes, the students with better study habits would be randomly distributed between the two groups. Now, if we see differences in scores on standardized tests between the two groups, this difference can be attributed to the only thing that is different about the two groups: one got advanced placement classes in high school and the other didn't. Random assignment to groups is the hallmark of a true experiment.

A quick word of caution—after years of teaching research methods, one of the most common errors we see students make is not understanding that random assignment to groups is not the same as using random sampling. *Random sampling* is done when you rely on chance to select participants for your study. By randomly selecting people to be in your study, you are ensuring that your findings are generalizable to the population from which they are sampled. *Random assignment* happens after you have selected people to be in your study. From your pool of participants, you may randomly assign some of them to get the independent variable and others to not get the independent variable. You can use random assignment to groups even if you did not use random sampling to select your participants and vice versa.

Randomized Posttest Design

The simplest true experiment is the *randomized posttest design* (see Figure 6.1). First, you obtain your sample using one of the methods described in Chapter 7. Then, you get two equivalent groups by randomly assigning half of your participants to the treatment group and half of your participants to the control group. The people in the treatment group then get the independent variable and the people in the control group do not. Finally, you measure the dependent variable in both groups. You then use a statistical test to see whether there is a difference between the treatment group and the control group on the dependent variable.

In our example, we would get a sample of high school students. We would randomly assign half of them to advanced placement classes and half to regular classes. Then, after the students complete their advanced placement classes, we would administer a standardized test. If our hypothesis is correct, we would find that the students who were in the advanced

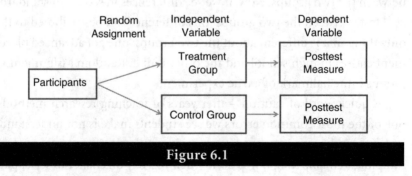

Figure 6.1

Randomized posttest design.

placement classes, on average, have higher scores on the standardized tests than the students who were in the regular classes.

Randomized Pretest–Posttest Design

The only difference between the randomized posttest design and the randomized pretest–posttest design (see Figure 6.2) is that the dependent variable is also measured before the independent variable is introduced. The advantage of using this design is that it allows you to check and make sure that your random assignment worked, and it also allows you to measure change over time. In other words, when you measure the independent variable at the beginning of the experiment, if you used random assignment to groups, you would expect to find that the groups are equivalent.

In our example, we would randomly assign students to the advanced placement classes or the regular classes. We would then measure their scores on a standardized test. We would expect the average test scores of students in the two groups to be equivalent at the beginning of the study. Then, the students in the treatment group would take advanced placement classes and the students in the control group would take regular classes. Finally, we would measure everyone's scores on a standardized test again. If the students in the treatment group have higher average test scores than the students in the control group, we have evidence that taking advanced placement classes causes higher standardized test scores.

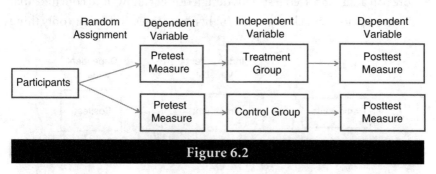

Figure 6.2

Randomized pretest–posttest design.

QUASI-EXPERIMENTS

Although true experiments do the best job of establishing internal validity, perhaps you have already noticed one of the biggest problems with this design: True experiments are not always possible! Would it really be ethical to take a group of high school kids and randomly assign half of them to advanced placement classes and half of them to regular classes? I'm pretty sure you'd get a lot of angry parents and students knocking on your door. When it is not possible to do a true experiment, you may want to consider using a quasi-experiment. Although a quasi-experiment might look a lot like an experiment, it is missing one of the essential elements of a true experiment—random assignment to groups. Therefore, you cannot be sure that the three criteria for establishing a causal relationship are met. There are many different quasi-experimental designs. We are going to cover a few of the most common ones. Quasi-experimental designs can be a good option if the purpose of your study is descriptive or exploratory.

One-Group Posttest Design

The one-group posttest design (see Figure 6.3) is one of the weakest quasi-experimental designs. In this design, participants are selected for the study, then receive the independent variable, and afterwards are tested on the dependent variable. In our example, we would have a group of high school kids who take advanced placement classes, and we would measure their scores on a standardized test. This design doesn't allow us to conclude that advanced placement classes cause higher test scores. In fact, the only thing

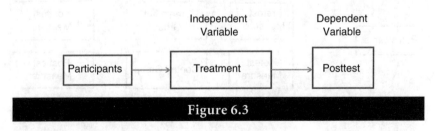

Figure 6.3

One-group posttest design.

we might be able to conclude is that taking advanced placement classes in high school may be correlated with test scores.

One-Group Pretest–Posttest Design

The one-group pretest–posttest design (see Figure 6.4) is similar to the one-group posttest design except that you add in a measurement point before the independent variable is introduced (pretest). You can then determine whether there is any change in scores from the pretest to the posttest. In our example, we would have a group of high school kids who are planning on taking advanced placement classes. We would measure their test scores before they take any advanced placement classes, and we would measure their test scores again after they completed the advanced placement classes. We would calculate the change in test scores from pretest to posttest and determine whether the test scores went up.

One of the notable problems with this design is that we can't be sure whether students' test scores went up because of taking advanced placement classes or simply because the students got a little older (maturation). In order to address this, we need to add a comparison group to our design.

Nonequivalent Groups Design

One of the most widely used quasi-experimental designs is the nonequivalent groups design (see Figure 6.5). It is a lot like the randomized pretest–posttest design, with one notable exception: It lacks random assignment to groups. Instead, in the nonequivalent groups design, you try to find two already existing groups that you think are very similar to one another.

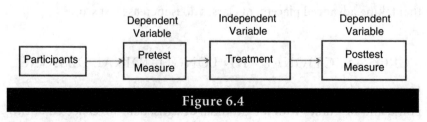

Figure 6.4

One-group pretest–posttest design.

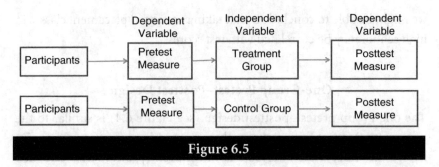

Figure 6.5

Nonequivalent groups design.

You then assign one group to receive the independent variable (treatment group) and one group to not receive the independent variable (control group). You measure the dependent variable in both groups before the treatment is administered (pretest) and again after the treatment is administered (posttest).

In our example, we would find a group of students who were planning on enrolling in advanced placement classes, and this would be our treatment group. We would try to find a group of students who are similar to our treatment group in every possible way (e.g., gender, socioeconomic status, study habits) except that they are not planning on taking advanced placement classes, and this would be our control group. We would have students in both groups take a standardized test. The treatment group would then take the advanced placement classes. Then, we would again have students in both groups take the standardized test again.

We might find that test scores went up in both groups. However, if the test scores go up more on average for the students in the treatment group as compared with the students in the control group, then we have evidence that taking advanced placement classes does increase test scores.

CROSS-SECTIONAL AND LONGITUDINAL DESIGNS

In studies with cross-sectional designs, data are collected at only one time point, and in studies with longitudinal designs, data are collected at two or more time points. Often the goal of longitudinal designs is to assess development or change over time. To truly study development (and determine developmental trajectories), a study must include at least three measurement time points. One of the most common longitudinal designs is called a *time series*. In this design, the same people are followed and measured at multiple time points. The participants are measured at baseline, before the independent variable is introduced, and again multiple times during and after the introduction of the independent variable.

QUALITATIVE DESIGNS

Unlike the various quantitative designs discussed previously in this chapter, qualitative designs are not as clear and distinguishable in their design elements, nor are they as connected to a specific study purpose. That is, almost any qualitative design can have an exploratory, descriptive, or explanatory purpose. There also is no intent for a qualitative study to demonstrate either generalizability or cause and effect, partly because of the nature of qualitative research itself, which allows the design to emerge as the study progresses rather than being completely prescribed and controlled before it begins.

For example, let's suppose you are conducting a qualitative study to understand the decision-making process for selecting incoming freshmen to participate in a new learning community program for psychology majors. The goal of the program is to mentor psychology majors who want to go to graduate school so that they graduate on time and successfully enter a graduate program. The reason for the study is that more than half of the psychology students switched majors and left the program, and of those remaining, most did not get into a graduate program. Obviously, this is a problem for the program and the students.

You decide to interview several admissions officers with the assumption that the admissions decision process was not correctly identifying students most likely to benefit from the program and be successful. Over the course of the interviews, several admissions officers mentioned that they heard students complaining about the lack of research opportunities in the program. At this point, you realize that maybe the problem is not with admissions, but with the program itself (i.e., you realized you shouldn't make assumptions). This new information must be followed. As a qualitative researcher, you are able to alter the design and focus midstudy. So you decide to hold several focus groups with former students and review documents contained in student files in hopes of figuring out the "real" problem.

If you look back at Table 4.1 in Chapter 4 and find the row labeled *Design* in the qualitative column, you will see a list of many design examples, including case study, grounded theory, narrative, and phenomenology, among others. In fact, there are many varieties of qualitative studies, and they share several design elements, including many of those presented above. Even the most advanced researchers find it difficult to keep track of everything. To start, we provide you with information to help you design a basic qualitative study that includes direct data collection from people, as opposed to content or textual data, and then we demonstrate a few more specific and common designs.

A Basic Qualitative Design

At its core, qualitative research seeks to gain depth of understanding about experiences, meaning, processes, and the like. Such understanding often is context and person dependent, meaning that you do not wish to generalize your findings beyond your sample or the context of an experience. To *gain depth* means you cannot reduce something to a number. Instead, you must seek to know everything about an experience. More crudely, rather than gathering a response of 4 to a survey question, for example, you would seek to understand what that 4 meant to the person who selected it and why he or she selected 4 as opposed to 3 or 5.

In Table 4.1 in Chapter 4, you were asked to put an X next to several characteristics of qualitative and quantitative approaches. Many characteristics in the qualitative column are key design elements. Table 6.1 has some of the same characteristics, as well as new ones, including a new column meant to help you design a basic qualitative study. The new column has a series of items for you to consider when designing your project. As you will see, the design of a qualitative project is more about the process. Importantly, always remember ethics when designing your project.

Table 6.1

Qualitative Design Characteristics and Considerations

General design characteristics	Characteristic definition	Design considerations
Bias and values	Acknowledgment of your own bias and values—that is, researcher subjectivity (e.g., be up-front about them; use reflexivity).	Reflect on who you are, your style of communication, your background, your cultural heritage, and your personal and professional views and beliefs about the topic you are studying.
		Consider how you react when people share something with you that is counter to your values and beliefs, and reflect on times when you have felt judged or marginalized.
		It might help to engage others in some of these reflections—use others as a mirror for yourself.
		Spend a great deal of time examining your biases and values before you begin the study, and continuously engage in reflection throughout the entire project.
		Keep a journal with your reflections.
Cultural competency	Cultivation of awareness and respect for the culture of your topic and of the participants in your sample. *Culture* can refer, for example, to a particular group of people (e.g., Asian Americans), a country (e.g., German culture), a context (e.g., poverty), or a set of practices (e.g., how holidays are celebrated in a family).	Read about the culture.
		Learn cultural languages, practices, and meanings.
		Identify someone or enlist an advisory board from that culture who can offer feedback. They can also help with question development or interpretation of data, although no one person can speak on behalf of an entire culture.
		Pilot test interview questions with someone.

(continues)

Table 6.1
Qualitative Design Characteristics and Considerations (*Continued*)

General design characteristics	Characteristic definition	Design considerations
Access and trust	Ways in which you gain trust and access to the community and groups of people you will study. Qualitative research often focuses on marginalized and/or highly specific groups.	Spend time in the community (this is also a way to learn about culture). Develop a relationship with someone in the community, and consider inviting them to be on the research team or advisory board. Make plans to give back to the community by providing incentives or sharing your findings in a public forum and with participants. Collect data in the community and other natural environments (e.g., in a participant's home).
Role of researcher	Development of a high level of interaction with participants and of strong rapport and trust.	View participants as the experts rather than yourself. Build in ways to get to know participants a little and interact with them a few times before collecting actual data (this can be done through some small talk and during scheduling of data collection). Ask participants what you can do to make it more comfortable to share. Be humble. Be nonjudgmental.
Depth	The extent to which your data accurately reflect all there is to know about an experience, process, or other area of interest.	Use multiple data collection procedures. Ensure trustworthiness (review Chapter 10).

Last, what should be evident across all of these general design characteristics is that the main design element for qualitative researchers is to establish a strong relationship with your participants, even before you meet them for the first time. This is fundamental to all qualitative research with humans.

Phenomenology

Phenomenology is one of the more common types of qualitative design. Its primary goal is to understand lived experience, and it is well suited to understanding emotions, processes, or reactions; this goal should be reflected in the research question. The research question can be anything from how new freshmen experience the psychology learning community program to how someone interprets the experience of falling in love on social media. Implicit in a phenomenological design is that the essence of an experience can be shared in some ways among a group of people and that your job is to uncover it. Most often phenomenological studies collect data primarily through interviews with individuals who share a similar experience or phenomenon. Studies also are highly focused and narrow in the selection of a phenomenon. To be successful, researchers must be aware of and set aside any preconceived notions, values, or beliefs about the phenomenon so they can fully attend to the experiences of their participants. This process is referred to as *bracketing* and is a key design element.

Narrative

Narrative studies focus most on stories. When solely in text form, narrative often is connected to a hermeneutical design. We all have stories of our lives and experiences. They are a great way to communicate with people, to share our experiences, or to teach. Just think about some of the classes in which you learned a great deal or about some of the professors whose teaching style you really enjoyed—we bet they were great storytellers.

Any good story has a plot, actors, interactions, context (i.e., the setting), and a time period. Accordingly, you should design your study in a way that allows you to gather data about each of these and reflect them in your research question. Although you could ask interview questions about each, we suggest also asking participants to share pictures, videos, social media posts, and so forth to help you get a deeper sense of the entire story (referred to as a form of *triangulation*; see Chapter 10). This strategy will allow you to see into their experiences and gather extremely detailed information.

Grounded Theory

Grounded theory is a pretty cool design that, in a basic sense, allows you to develop a theory to explain something in which you are interested. It truly is an emergent design in that you develop a theory that emerges from the data rather than using an existing theory to explain your data. Studies of this type almost always include several different types of data (e.g., interviews with different people, journal writings, observations). Analysis occurs during data collection and directs the next types of data you need to collect (referred to as *theoretical sampling*).

As the theory begins to emerge, it leads you to new questions to ask and answer to build your theory. Thus, you constantly compare your data as you collect it and then identify a core category. The *core category* can be thought of as the one concept that is at the center of your theory and to which every other concept in your theory is connected. Using visual concept maps is a helpful technique to track the analysis and watch your theory emerge. You can even think about all the articles you read for your research project as data in developing your emergent theory!

For example, you might read a lot of research studies about children's experience with their parents' divorce (topic of literature review and core concept) and realize that there are a group of studies that discuss findings related to how divorce impacts children's academic achievement, peer relationships, stress and anxiety levels, and so on. These are additional concepts that give you information about the core concept. You also realize that many of the articles talk about how anxiety levels among these children affect their academic achievement. This is an example of an emergent theoretical link between concepts. These all can be used as headings and subheadings to organize the literature review and tell the story of children's experiences when their parents divorce.

Case Study

A case study has many similarities with other designs, but what really sets it apart is that it is *bounded*. *Bounding* is when the researcher sets clear criteria for the boundaries that define their case (i.e., what or who is and is not a case). For example, the researcher might identify a specific person, a specific type of family, a specific hospital, or a specific university as the participant in the case. The more specific and narrow the case, the better. You might be familiar with case studies involving single individuals (a bounded case of one person), such as those presented by doctors or psychologists when discussing a patient with a unique illness or a particularly challenging client being treated.

Case study research might result in a detailed account of a person and his or her response to a novel treatment approach. It also could describe one student's experience in the psychology learning community. Alternatively, it could describe the experience of all students in the learning community; in this situation the case study would describe the learning community from the perspective of the students, rather than the students themselves. You could even do a case study on everyone in your class doing their first research project. The *unit of analysis*—person versus learning community versus class—should be clear for a project to be called a case study.

Ethnography and Autoethnography

Ethnographies seek to understand culture. The ethnography design is extremely time intensive; many ethnographers live in the community they are studying for months or even years, referred to as an *immersion process*. This process is similar to what some believe is the best way to learn a new language: to be dropped off in the middle of a city in a country where the language is spoken and to survive for a month on one's own. You would be amazed at how quickly you can pick up a new language in this way! The belief is that to understand culture, one must experience it in the field firsthand during data collection. Journaling, intensive observation, and field notes are important elements of this design.

A spin on ethnography is autoethnography. This is a fairly new method to many disciplines, and it is still debated as a method by some. In many ways it is similar to ethnography, as you would expect. The key difference is that the researcher is also the participant. That is, *autoethnography* is the study of one's self. For example, you could critically examine how you were able to survive your first research project. When using this design, it is most helpful to use some type of document you have maintained (e.g., journal, emails) as data and to plan to interview several people who know you to gain their perceptions. This type of data naturally allows for triangulation and helps manage potential bias. We warn you that this can be a highly emotional endeavor, and projects can be stalled for months at a time because of the difficulty of reliving a personal experience or seeing parts of our life more clearly and in ways we didn't see them before.

CASE STUDY: DR. HERTZOG, PART 1

Exhibit 6.1 presents a research topic to explore. How should the study be designed? Read the case, answer the questions, and discuss your answers with other students.

APPLYING CONCEPTS TO YOUR RESEARCH PROPOSAL

Now you are ready to write the Design section of your research proposal. Describe the type of design you will use to conduct your study. For a quantitative study, determine whether you will be doing a true experiment or a quasi-experiment. Remember, in order to do a true experiment, you must be able to randomly assign participants to groups. If you are able to do a true experiment, explain how participants will be assigned to treatment and control groups and what will happen to each group. If you are conducting a quasi-experiment, specify which design you will use (e.g., one-group posttest-only design, nonequivalent groups design, time-series design). State whether you will have one group or multiple groups (note that

> ## Exhibit 6.1
>
> ### Case Study of Dr. Hertzog, Part 1
>
> Dr. Hertzog is working on designing a study. She has noticed that some working women choose to return to work after the birth of their first child, whereas other working women decide to leave the paid workforce after the birth of their first child. She is interested in knowing more about these women's general life satisfaction after the birth of the child. She hypothesizes that new mothers who had been working prior to the birth of their first child will be more satisfied with life if they do not return to work after the birth of their child compared with new mothers who return to work.
>
> 1. What is the independent variable, and what is the dependent variable?
> 2. What type of design would you suggest to Dr. Hertzog? Should she do an experiment, quasi-experiment, or a nonexperiment?
> 3. Would you suggest that that she use a quantitative, qualitative, or mixed-methods approach? Why?
> 4. Would you suggest that she use a cross-sectional or a longitudinal design? Why?
>
> *Answers:* 1. return to work (independent), general life satisfaction (dependent); 2. name a specific design and explain; 3. suggest a specific approach; 4. select one and describe why you selected it.

multiple-group designs are stronger and are highly encouraged). Explain how you will decide who is in which group.

For a qualitative study, explain the research paradigm you will be applying and the rationale for using that approach (e.g., naturalism, ethnography, grounded theory, case study). Explain the role you will play as an observer and your relations with the people you will be observing. In a sentence or two, explain whether your study is cross-sectional or longitudinal and whether you will use primary data or secondary data. If it is longitudinal, specify when measurements will be taken.

7

Choosing Your Sample

Determining your sample and your sampling strategy is an important decision in designing your research study. On the surface, selecting people to be in your study may seem like a pretty straightforward process. It is and it isn't. Careful thought needs to go into deciding how you will select people. There are many different strategies that can be used, and the one you pick has important ramifications. You're probably wondering what the different options are. Before we get to that, it's important to go over some terminology first. Let's get started!

UNIT OF ANALYSIS VERSUS UNIT OF OBSERVATION

You need to begin by thinking about the focus of your research. Are you interested in individuals, groups such as cliques or classrooms, schools, states, or some other entity? The level your research question focuses on is called the *unit of analysis*. It is important to determine what unit of analysis

http://dx.doi.org/10.1037/0000049-007
Designing and Proposing Your Research Project, by J. B. Urban and B. M. van Eeden-Moorefield

your research question focuses on. Consider the following example: Dr. Kulkofsky is interested in whether first graders who express empathy are more likely to engage in prosocial behaviors (helping others). She collects data from individual children on the extent to which they express empathy and on the extent to which they engage in prosocial behaviors. She analyzes the relationship between empathy and prosocial behaviors to see whether children who express more empathy also engage in more prosocial behaviors. The data describe individuals, and individuals are the unit of analysis.

In some studies, groups are the unit of analysis, but data are collected from individuals. Dr. Klemfuss hypothesizes that classes that use the Happy Phonics reading program will have higher reading proficiency scores than classes that do not use the program. Reading proficiency is measured by giving each of the individual students a test. However, the individual student test scores are averaged to create an average score for each classroom. Then, classrooms that used Happy Phonics are compared with classrooms that did not use Happy Phonics. The differences in classroom average scores are used to explain variation in reading proficiency. The data describe individuals, but classrooms are the unit of analysis.

The *unit of observation* is the level at which the data are actually collected. It's important to distinguish between the unit of analysis and the unit of observation. In Dr. Klemfuss's study, data were collected from individuals, which were the units of observation, and then the data were aggregated and analyzed at the group level, which was the unit of analysis. In some studies, the unit of analysis and the unit of observation are the same, as in Dr. Kulkofsky's study.

POPULATION VERSUS SAMPLE

For a quantitative study, the goal is to select a sample that is representative of the population so that the results of the study are generalizable. For a qualitative study, the objective is not typically to obtain a sample that is representative of the population. Rather, the objective is to obtain a sample that can most appropriately address your research question.

Imagine you pick up your college newspaper and read a story about an amazing new GRE prep course being offered at your college. In the article, the reporter describes an interview he did with one of the students at your college who had tried studying on her own but was never able to get a high enough score to get into her dream graduate program. The article goes on to explain how the GRE prep course taught her amazing tips and tricks that helped her get the score she needed. The article then goes on to describe another success story of a student who had tried other GRE prep courses to no avail and was finally able to raise his score after taking the new GRE prep course.

Sounds great, right? Only problem is that you don't know whether the two people described in the story are like most of the students who have taken the prep course, most students at your college, or most college students in your state or across the country or whether they're just two students who happened to be willing to talk to the newspaper reporter. In other words, you don't know whether their experience is generalizable to other students. This unknown is particularly problematic if your goal is to understand whether the GRE prep course would be helpful for most students.

So, how could you figure out whether this GRE prep course is really as amazing as it sounds or is too good to be true? Well, you could interview everyone in the country who took the GRE prep course and compare them with those who didn't take the course, but that would be a lot of people and way too much work. What you need to do is interview a sample (or subset) of those people. The main thing you need to make sure of is that your sample is representative of the larger group you are interested in saying something about because your study will be quantitative.

Let's take another example. Imagine you want to study the impact of high-stakes testing in elementary schools in the United States. Ultimately, your goal is to be able to say something about all elementary schools in the United States, so your population is U.S. elementary schools. Or you might have another study in which you want to be able to say something about all residents of New Jersey or all articles published in *The New York Times* between 2010 and 2015. These are all examples of your *population* of interest, or the entire set of things, people, or groups about which you want to say something.

Typically, it's not feasible to conduct a study on the entire population of interest. You'll need to select a sample or subset of the population. Your sample might be a subset of elementary schools in the United States, a subset of New Jersey residents, or a subset of articles published in *The New York Times* between 2010 and 2015.

When you select a sample for a quantitative study, you are doing so in the hopes that your sample is representative of the larger population. That way, you can generalize the findings from the sample in your study back to the larger population the sample was drawn from. So, how can you be sure that your sample is actually representative of the population? Well, the first step is to define the *sampling frame*, or the list of all of the elements in the population of interest. Your sampling frame might be a list of all elementary schools in the United States, a list of all New Jersey residents, or a list of all articles published in *The New York Times* between 2010 and 2015.

Sometimes it's easier to develop an accurate sampling frame than others. It would be relatively easy to create a list of all articles published in *The New York Times* in a certain period. It would be less easy, though still doable, to create a list of all elementary schools in the United States. It would actually be pretty difficult to put together a list of all New Jersey residents. Researchers used to be able to use phone books to generate sampling frames, but have you seen a phone book recently, or do you even have a landline?

Remember that the ultimate goal in quantitative research is drawing a sample that is representative of the population of interest. You do this so that your findings from your sample can be generalized to the population from which the sample was drawn. If you want to say something about high-stakes testing in all U.S. elementary schools, then your sample has to be representative of all U.S. elementary schools. Your sample could not include only elementary schools in New Jersey. Why not? Well, New Jersey elementary schools are probably not representative of all elementary schools in the United States. Sometimes you are actually able to avoid the issue of generalizability completely by doing a *census*, which is when you study the entire population of interest. This is what the federal government does every 10 years with the U.S. Census. Most of the time, you are not able to conduct a census, and you need to select a sample.

Despite your best efforts, you usually won't be able to draw a perfectly representative sample. When this happens, it's called *sampling error,* or the difference between the characteristics of the population and the sample that was actually drawn. The greater the sampling error, the less representative your sample is of the larger population from which it was drawn.

SAMPLING STRATEGIES

Remember that in quantitative research, your objective is to select a sample that is as representative of your population of interest as possible. If you want to be able to say something about all third graders in Wisconsin but you can't actually study all third graders in Wisconsin, you want to make sure your sample is representative of all third graders in Wisconsin.

Recall that in qualitative research, your objective is to select a sample that can most appropriately address the research question; therefore, a more targeted sampling approach is often needed. There are two major sampling strategies you can use to select your sample: probability sampling techniques, which are most commonly used in quantitative studies, and nonprobability sampling techniques, which are most commonly used in qualitative studies. Probability sampling techniques rely on random chance in selecting a sample, so you know that every element in the population has a known *probability*, or chance, of being selected. Nonprobability sampling techniques, on the other hand, do not rely on chance, and you don't know the probability of any element in a population being selected. There are several specific techniques that can be used when doing probability and nonprobability sampling. Table 7.1 summarizes some of the most common techniques, which we will now go over one at a time.

Probability Sampling Techniques

Imagine that your high school has just initiated a tobacco prevention campaign, and the administration wants to get a sense of how many high school students are using tobacco products. In order to figure this out, the principal decides to conduct a survey of all of the high school students.

Table 7.1		
Sampling Techniques		
Technique	How it is done	When it is used
Probability sampling techniques		
Simple random sampling	Participants are randomly selected from the population.	Used when a complete sampling frame is available
Systematic random sampling	Participants are randomly selected from a sequential list or files.	Used when a complete but large sampling frame is available
Stratified random sampling	Participants are divided into groups on the basis of some characteristic, and some number are then randomly selected from each group.	Used when a complete sampling frame is available and the researcher determines it is crucial that members of different groups be included
Cluster random sampling	Clusters within a population are identified, and some clusters are randomly selected. Participants are then randomly selected from the set of selected clusters.	Used when a list of clusters or geographic areas is available but the researcher lacks access to lists of elements within clusters
Nonprobability sampling techniques		
Convenience sampling	Participants are selected on the basis of availability.	Used when other sampling approaches cannot be used and occasionally for pilot studies
Quota sampling	The population is divided into subgroups; participants are selected from within subgroups on the basis of convenience.	Used when the researcher determines it is crucial that members of different groups be included but they cannot be selected randomly
Snowball sampling	Participants are selected on the basis of referrals from other participants.	Used to study hard-to-reach populations
Purposive sampling	Participants are selected according to researchers' judgment and for a specific reason.	Used when the researcher knows a lot about the population of interest and wants to collect information from a clearly defined group

The problem is that there are 5,067 students in the high school, and it would take too much time away from classwork to survey all of them. Instead, the principal decides to draw a sample from the high school population to participate in the survey. He figures that surveying about 250 students should be plenty.

The vice principal points out that there are about 250 students taking drama classes, and it wouldn't be a big deal if the students missed a drama class, so why not just survey them? Well, this strategy could affect the results because kids who choose to take drama classes might tend to smoke more or less than other kids. So then the vice principal suggests that members of the student council distribute surveys to students in the hall as they're walking to the cafeteria for lunch. What's wrong with this approach? Well, any student who is willing to stop and take a survey on the way to lunch is probably not a smoker looking to get a nicotine fix during the lunch break. The best sampling strategy would not give any particular student, or category of student, a better chance of being selected than any other student. In other words, we need a sampling strategy that gives every student an equal and known chance of being included.

So, what did the principal in this example decide to do? Well, he realized that all students are required to take health class, and he wasn't concerned about giving over one health class session for a survey. So he got a list of all of the health classes. He knew that each class had about 25 students in it. He randomly selected 10 health classes to participate in the survey. Because every student in the school was enrolled in a health class and every class had an equal chance of being selected, the principal knew that every student had an equal and known chance of being selected to participate and that he had drawn a representative sample.

Simple Random Sampling

One of the most common and easiest probability sampling techniques is simple random sampling. This is a technique in which every element in the population has an equal chance of being selected for the sample. How can you do it? Imagine that your population of interest is the students in your research methods class, and you want to make sure that every student in your class has an equal chance of being in your study. The only problem is that you can include only five students in the study. You could have every student write their name on a piece of paper and put the papers in a bowl. You could select a simple random sample by drawing out five names to be included in your study. That's a pretty low-tech way to draw a simple random sample. You could get a little more sophisticated by listing your classmates' names in an Excel file and using a random number generator to randomly sort the names and select five.

Systematic Random Sampling

A slightly more sophisticated probability sampling technique, systematic random sampling, is especially useful when you have a sampling frame that is ordered sequentially, such as patient files at a doctor's office. In this technique, the sample is selected from a sequential list or files. Imagine that you work in a social service agency that has files for all 500 of its clients (the population). Say you wanted to conduct a study on your client population but you have funding to study only 100 clients (the sample). You could use systematic random sampling to select every 10th file to be in your sample. In this example, 10 is your *sampling interval*, or the number of files between one sampled file and the next sampled file.

Key to this approach is selecting the starting point randomly. You have 500 total folders, so randomly select a number between 1 and 500. Let's say you randomly selected the number 22. So, count to the 22nd folder in your filing cabinet, and pull that folder out. That's the first client in your sample. Remember that your sampling interval is 10, so count 10 folders from where you are and pull out the 10th folder. That's the next client in your sample. Count 10 more folders and pull that one out, and so on until you've drawn out 100 client folders.

Stratified Random Sampling

It's important to keep in mind that the research question and hypothesis should guide your decisions when designing your study; this is particularly true when selecting a sample. Your university, like most, probably has an alumni network. When you graduate, you'll learn that just because you have your degree in hand doesn't mean that you won't hear from your university again. Probably about every year, you'll get a phone call (perhaps from a current student) asking you to donate money to your alma mater. Now, imagine that the president of your university is about to institute a major change to the organization of the colleges, but she doesn't want to upset the alumni who provide important financial resources for the university. So before she institutes any changes, she decides to conduct a survey. She has to rely on the list of alumni who are already active donors to the university. That list contains about 10,000 names. The president knows that most alumni donors give $500 or less a year, but there is a smaller group of alumni donors (about 300) who give substantially more. Because the smaller donors outnumber the substantial donors, using a simple random sample would likely result in very few (if any) big money donors. The president wants to make sure that the voices of the big donors are included in the survey. In this example, using a stratified random sample would be ideal. This technique is especially useful when you know that there is a minority group in the population and including their perspective is important to addressing the research question.

In the example above, the president could create a stratified random sample by first dividing (stratifying) the population (alumni donors) into two groups based on whether each donor is a large or small donor. This would essentially create two sampling frames: a list of big donors and a list of small donors (see Figure 7.1). The sample would include alumni drawn from each group.

Once the president divided (stratified) her sample, the next decision she needs to make is how many names to draw from each sampling frame. Let's say that Sampling Frame A, which includes the list of small donors, has 9,700 names and that Sampling Frame B, which includes the list of big donors, has 300 names. She might decide to select the same proportion of people from each sampling frame. This is known as *probability proportionate to size* sampling. In other words, if she selects 10% of people from Sampling Frame A, she would also select 10% of people from Sampling Frame B.

Imagine that the president selected 10% from each sampling frame. She would end up with 970 people from Sampling Frame A (small donors)

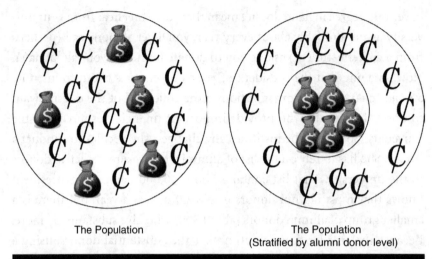

The Population

The Population
(Stratified by alumni donor level)

Figure 7.1

Stratified random sample.

and only 30 people from Sampling Frame B (big donors). There wouldn't be enough people from Sampling Frame B to make meaningful comparisons. So, what can she do? She could *oversample*, or select a higher proportion of people from Sampling Frame B. In other words, she might select 5% of people from Sampling Frame A (485 people) and 80% of people from Sampling Frame B (240 people).

Now you give it a try. Imagine that the students in your research methods class comprise your population of interest and that it's really important for your research question that you have an adequate number of sophomores in your sample, so you decide to draw a stratified random sample. You ask all of the sophomores to stand up and gather on the right side of the classroom. You ask everyone else to gather on the left side of the classroom. You immediately notice that in a class of 30 students you have only eight sophomores and that you're going to have to oversample sophomores. You decide that you want to select five sophomores and five students from the group of freshmen, juniors, and seniors to be in your study.

You ask all of the students to write their name on a piece of paper. First, you walk over to the group of sophomores on the right side of the room.

You ask them to put their slips of paper in the bowl, and you randomly draw out five names to be part of your sample. Then you empty the bowl and walk over to the other group of students on the left side of the room. You ask them to put their slips of paper in the bowl, and you randomly draw out five names to also be part of your sample. And there you have it. You've successfully drawn a stratified random sample.

Cluster Random Sampling

So far, all of the strategies have required that you have a complete sampling frame before selecting the sample. Sometimes this isn't available, and you may need to use a multistage sampling approach, one of which is cluster sampling. Many populations are actually made up of clusters. For example, the individuals who comprise the population of fourth graders are clustered within schools. In order to draw a cluster random sample, first you need to randomly select the clusters, and then you need to randomly select individuals from within the selected clusters.

Suppose the governor of New Jersey has asked you to conduct a study that compares the experiences of first-year students enrolled in community colleges in the state with those of first-year students enrolled in state-funded 4-year colleges. You discover that although each institution has its own list of first-year students, there is no such thing as a complete list of all first-year college students in New Jersey. New Jersey has 45 institutions of higher learning, and the thought of putting together the 45 lists of names to create one big sampling frame is rather daunting, not to mention it won't be easy to convince the registrars of each of those institutions to hand over their enrollment lists. But you have a plan!

First, you take the list of 45 colleges and assign each a number. Then you randomly select some number of those colleges to be part of your study. You contact the registrars of each of the selected schools, and you obtain a list of enrolled first-year students. Next, you draw a random number of students from each list, and this is your sample. Note that you didn't need to get the list of students from all 45 institutions, but only from those schools that were randomly selected. Also, note that each student at each of those 45 colleges had an equal and known chance of being selected.

Assuming that the enrollment lists are accurate, you have successfully drawn a representative sample from the population of 45 New Jersey institutions of higher education.

Nonprobability Sampling Techniques

It is not always possible or desirable to use a probability sampling approach. Imagine that you want to study adolescent depression. How easy would it be to find a list of adolescents with depressive symptoms? Sometimes you're actually not interested in finding a representative sample. At times, you might be interested in a very specific group of people, or you're not sure who you actually want in your sample and you need to use an approach that helps you identify members of the population of interest. Whatever the case may be, it's important to remember that when a nonprobability sampling technique is used, you can't be confident that your results will be generalizable to a larger population.

Convenience Sampling

Have you ever been at the mall and had someone walk up to you and ask if you would be willing to answer a couple of questions for a research or marketing study? Social media sites and magazines frequently survey their readers. Have you ever responded to a quiz on social media or read a magazine that contained a questionnaire that asked readers to respond and submit their answers? This was likely followed by an article with a title such as "What You Think About Dating and Hooking Up!"

This might seem like a good approach to research, but alas, it's not. This approach relies on *convenience sampling*, which is the least defensible sampling approach. What's the problem? Well, remember that one of the first things you want to do when drawing a sample is to determine the population. With convenience sampling, there is no definable population from which to draw the sample. The second thing you want to do is use a systematic approach to select respondents. Here again, convenience sampling falls short. The people who happen to be available and have time to answer survey questions at the mall are probably not just like the people who are unavailable. In fact, the kind of people who are likely to show up at a mall are probably not a lot like those who tend to rely on Amazon for most of their shopping. Using this approach, you can't be sure that what you learn from your respondents at the mall can be generalized to a broader population.

You run into the same problem with a social media or magazine quiz. Usually only a small fraction of the people who see the quiz will actually respond to it. The people who take the time to fill out the quiz (if you spend all day on social media, you know who you are) are probably not the same as those who don't have the time or interest in taking the quiz. So, here again, you have an example of a convenience sample.

Now you give it a try. Imagine again that you want to do a survey of students at your university. You know that you have research methods class this afternoon, so you ask your professor if you can ask a few students to complete a short survey. You sit down in your usual spot in the first row, and you hand the survey out to the other students who are also sitting in the first row with you. What's wrong with this approach? How might the students sitting in the first row be different from other students in the class?

Despite its many drawbacks, convenience sampling may be appropriate if you are trying to explore a new setting or if you are conducting a pilot (or preliminary) study in which you are trying to test a new set of questions. It also can work fairly well for qualitative studies. In general, though, if you do need to use a nonprobability sampling technique, there are some other better options.

Quota Sampling

Do you remember when we talked about stratified random sampling? *Quota sampling* is the nonprobability version of that. Just as with stratified random sampling, the researcher knows that there are some important differences or groups within the population (e.g., big donors and small donors). The population is stratified (or divided) on the basis of those groups. Remember that in the stratified random sampling example, the university president randomly selected people from each group (some number of big donors and some number of small donors). However, in quota sampling, rather than randomly selecting elements from each group, you would select elements on the basis of convenience or for a specific reason. For example, you might call just participants who have local phone numbers in order to save money on long-distance phone charges.

Now you try it. The students in your research methods class are your population of interest, and it's really important for your research question that you have an adequate number of sophomores in your sample. You ask all of the sophomores to stand up and gather on the right side of the classroom. You ask everyone else to gather on the left side of the classroom. You decide that you want to select five sophomores and five students from the group of freshmen, juniors, and seniors to be in your study. First, you walk over to the group of sophomores on the right side of the room, and you point to the five students you always eat lunch with. Then you walk over to the other group of students on the left side of the room, and you point to the five students who live in your dorm. And there you have it. You've just drawn a quota sample.

Snowball Sampling

In snowball sampling, you begin by identifying someone in your population of interest. You then ask that person to give you the name and contact information for another person in that population, and then you ask that person to identify another person, and so on. A second strategy is to ask a participant to share your contact information with others they know who might also be interested in participating; this is less intrusive than the first strategy and can be a good choice, although it is a bit riskier of a decision. When this second strategy is paired with another strategy, the risk decreases, and you can have the best of both worlds (low intrusion, greater access to potential participants who fit the study criteria).

Snowball sampling is often used when the researcher is interested in studying members of marginalized or hidden populations. These are people who may want to keep their identity confidential. For example, they could be drug users, criminals, people with a certain disease, or members of Gamblers Anonymous. When snowball sampling is used, the researcher cannot be sure that the sample is representative of the larger population. One of the biggest criticisms of this technique is that the entire sample can be shaped by the initial contact. However, this technique can be invaluable when working with hard-to-reach populations.

You give it a try. Select a student in your class, and ask them to pick another student. Now go to that student and ask them to pick another student, and so on until you have the desired number of students in your sample.

Purposive Sampling

In purposive sampling, all of the elements of the sample are selected for a clear purpose. This sampling technique is most useful when the researcher knows a lot about the population of interest, and it's one of the most common, and strongest, strategies for qualitative studies. It's important to recognize that purposive sampling does not produce a representative sample; however, it can be exactly what is needed when you're trying to sample from a clearly defined group. Remember that purposive sampling is not the same as convenience sampling. You're not picking the sample because it's convenient; you're picking it because it fulfills some clearly defined need or has specific characteristics of interest.

Imagine that we are interested in studying differences between socioeconomically diverse communities compared with more homogenous communities. We know of three towns in our county that are very socioeconomically diverse and three other towns that are very homogeneous, one with residents with low socioeconomic status, one with residents who are middle class, and one with residents with high socioeconomic status. We select these six towns because they clearly meet the specific needs of our study.

Using Multiple Sampling Techniques

Sometimes you may find that you need to use more than one type of sampling strategy in order to generate the sample for your study. For instance, use the example we gave above for drawing a purposive sample of six towns. Although we used a purposive sampling technique to select those six towns, we may then decide to use cluster random sampling to select three elementary schools from each town and then six classes from each of the randomly selected schools. This layered sampling approach is frequently used, and it is important to describe the sampling approach used at each phase in your report.

SAMPLE QUALITY

There are several important things to consider when determining whether the sample is of high quality or not. First, the quality of the sample is based on the sample that is actually obtained, not just the type of sampling technique that was used. For example, if a lot of people don't agree to participate in your study, it is important to consider whether all of the people who refused to participate shared some sort of underlying characteristic (e.g., they were mostly female). This is a particularly important thing to consider if you use a probability sampling technique. You cannot assume that your sample is representative of the larger population if there is considerable systematic nonresponse.

When determining the quality of a sample, remember that you can evaluate its quality only if you know the population that it is intended to represent. Finally, remember that it is important to know what sampling technique was used to select the sample. Without this information, you cannot assess the quality of the sample.

SAMPLE SIZE

Determining the sample size you need partly depends on whether you are conducting a study that is primarily quantitative or qualitative. For a quantitative study, you may be asked to conduct a *power analysis*, which helps determine how large a sample you need in order to detect an effect of a specified size with a specified degree of confidence. Sound complicated? If you've already taken a statistics class, you may already have learned about power analysis. There are many power analysis calculators available for free online (simply type *power analysis calculator* into your favorite search engine).

If power analysis sounds a bit overwhelming, you can follow this general rule for determining the sample needed for a quantitative study: You should have at least 30 people in each group. For example, if you have one treatment group and one control group, you should have a total of at least 60 people in your study. If there are no groups, you can use the general rule of 30 people for each variable.

For many qualitative studies, your goal is to reach *saturation*; you have achieved this once you are no longer hearing new things from participants. Determining the sample size for a qualitative study at the outset can be challenging. You should consult the literature on your topic to get a sense of how many participants have been needed in other similar studies. Generally, planning for a sample of 10 to 20 is a good bet. However, there are some designs (e.g., autoethnography, some case studies) in which a sample size of one—yes, one—is appropriate. Although these designs sound like they would make research easier, they actually can be much more time involved, and samples often include many types of documents in addition to the one person.

RECRUITMENT

In addition to thinking about how many people you will try and recruit for your study, you also need to think about how you will go about recruiting them. Where are you most likely to find potential participants? Are you interested in studying preschool children who may go to a school or day-care center on your campus? Are you interested in studying recent immigrants who may attend English as a second language classes at the local community center?

What's the best way of getting potential participants' attention? Perhaps you could post a recruitment flier with information about your study. Or you could send out an email announcement to a listserv. You may even be able to use social media platforms such as Facebook to reach your target population.

As you make decisions about recruiting participants, be sure to consider the potential ethical implications as well as challenges you may face. For example, studying children typically involves having to get consent from both the children and their parents (in addition to permission from the school). If you will actually conduct your research study, think about what you can feasibly do in a semester or a year. See Figure 7.2 for an example of a recruitment flyer.

Start with an eye-catching phrase, possibly include some eligibility criteria and graphics:

Are you a new mom? Are you thinking about returning to work?
Research Participants wanted.

Include a short description of the study, what will happen, how much time it will take, and where it will take place:

- We are looking at how new moms make decisions about returning to work.
- This study will take 30 minutes, during one session, at the REDSS Lab on the MSU Campus.
- Participants will receive a $10 gift card.

Provide a short description of who is conducting the study and how to reach them:

Sarah Hertzog and Heather Gilmore, Professors in the Human Development Department, are conducting this study. If you are interested in participating or have more questions, please contact them at (973) 555-1212 or momstudy@mail.montclair.edu

This study has been approved by the Montclair State University institutional review board.

Figure 7.2

Sample recruitment flyer for Dr. Hertzog's study.

CASE STUDY: DR. GILMORE, PART 2

Now it's time to return to our case study. You may want to reread Part 1 of Dr. Gilmore's case study, in Exhibit 5.5. Read Part 2 in Exhibit 7.1 and answer the questions. Check your answers with a colleague.

APPLYING CONCEPTS TO YOUR RESEARCH PROPOSAL

Now you're ready to think through and draft the sampling section of your research proposal. Write a short paragraph describing your basic sampling plan. Be sure to answer the following six questions:

1. What is the population of interest, and what is the sample you will use to study them?
2. What will your unit of analysis be? Will you be studying individual children, students, parents, couples, families, classrooms, schools, or neighborhoods?
3. How many participants (individuals, parents, couples, families, classrooms, schools, or neighborhoods) will you try to include in your sample? In other words, what is your sample size?
4. How and where will you find your participants?
5. What sampling strategy will you use to select participants (e.g., random selection, cluster random sampling, purposive sampling)?
6. What procedures might you follow when recruiting participants for your study? For your research proposal, you will need to be quite specific about procedures. For now, start by writing down your initial ideas, even if they are not completely detailed or you are not sure it is the actual strategy you will use.

Exhibit 7.1

Case Study of Dr. Gilmore, Part 2

Recall that Dr. Gilmore hypothesized that youth who spend more time in extracurricular activities will exhibit lower levels of risk-taking behaviors than youth who spend little or no time in extracurricular activities (see Part 1 of the case study in Exhibit 5.5). She has decided to conduct a study to test her hypothesis and needs help developing a sampling strategy. Ideally, she would like to be able to generalize her results to all high-school-age youth in the United States; however, her budget is limited, so she has decided to start smaller. In this initial study, Dr. Gilmore decides that she would like to generalize her results to all high school students in New Jersey.

1. What is the population in Dr. Gilmore's study?
2. What sampling strategy would you suggest to Dr. Gilmore, and why?
3. How would you suggest she go about recruiting the sample for her study?
4. What is the unit of analysis?
5. What is the unit of observation? Is the unit of analysis the same as the unit of observation?

Answers: 1. all high school students in New Jersey; 2. name a specific sampling approach and explain; 3. describe a recruitment strategy; 4. individuals; 5. individuals are the unit of observation, and yes, the unit of analysis is the same as the unit of observation.

8

Planning Your Measurement Strategy for Collecting Data

D ata can take many forms in both qualitative and quantitative research. In fact, researchers often view everything and everyone as sources of data, even ourselves! The main goal is to collect quality data (i.e., reliable and valid data for quantitative studies, and trustworthy data for qualitative studies) that can answer your research questions and hypotheses. A second goal is that any technique you use should not overburden those who take part in your study. In other words, taking part in the research process should not take an overly long time such that people become fatigued, drop out of the study, or get frustrated and annoyed. There are a few common ways you, as a new researcher, will collect data, and these are the focus of this chapter.

http://dx.doi.org/10.1037/0000049-008
Designing and Proposing Your Research Project, by J. B. Urban and B. M. van Eeden-Moorefield

SURVEYS

Surveys are probably the most commonly used form of quantitative data collection, and they often require minimal interaction between the researcher and participant. Surveys can be given in several forms: paper and pencil, verbally, or online. They also can be given using several modalities: in person, computer mediated (i.e., answered on a computer in a room with a researcher present), online, or via telephone. So, how do you decide? Table 8.1 provides some helpful hints to get you started.

As you can see in the table, all types of surveys have benefits and drawbacks. Consider a few additional things to help you make the best decision:

- The more sensitive the topic being studied (e.g., drug use, sexual behavior), the better it is to use a computer.
- The more you need to control the setting in which the survey is completed (e.g., by eliminating distractions), the better it is to give an in-person survey.
- The more important it is to reduce human error, the better it is to use a computer.
- The more time needed to complete a survey, the better it is to use a computer, or at least avoid verbal surveys.
- The easier the access you have to a sample (e.g., participant pool at your university), the more you should consider an in-person survey.

Levels of Measurement

By now, you hopefully know what variables you will study and what type of survey you will use. It's time to begin making decisions about how you will actually measure your variables. Before picking a measure or writing your own questions, it is important to review the following levels of measurement:

- *Nominal* variables are measured using categories. Survey questions might have response options that are dichotomous (yes or no) or categorical or polytomous (African American, Asian American, Native American, White). We artificially assign numbers to these categories

Table 8.1

Survey Strategy Choices and Benefits

Modality	Form	Benefits	Drawbacks
In person	Paper and pencil	Provides convenience for the researcher	Requires data entry, which could lead to errors
		Provides moderate confidentiality	Costs money to make copies
		Can be used for any topic	Places moderate demand on respondents' time
		Can be used to collect data from many people at once (efficient)	
		Is faster for the respondent to complete	
		Allows control over setting conditions	
In person	Verbally	Provides convenience for researcher	Requires recording and entry of data, which can lead to errors
		Allows control over setting conditions	Allows data collection from only one person at a time
		Does not depend on participants' reading abilities	Does not provide confidentiality, so not appropriate for measuring sensitive topics
			Places high demand on respondents' time
In person	Computer mediated	Provides convenience	Requires a research computer
		Provides fair confidentiality	Requires a survey program
		Can be used for any topic, including more sensitive topics	Places moderate demand on respondents' time
		Is faster for the respondent to complete	
		Requires no data entry	
		Allows control over setting conditions	

(continues)

Table 8.1

Survey Strategy Choices and Benefits (*Continued*)

Modality	Form	Benefits	Drawbacks
Telephone	Verbally	Provides access to people anywhere Can be more convenient for respondents	Requires recording and entry of data, which can lead to errors Allows data collection from only one person at a time Provides low confidentiality, so is not appropriate for sensitive topics Places high demand on respondents' time Provides access only to people with phones Requires access to phone numbers Makes it easier for respondents not to participate Does not allow control over setting conditions
Online	Computer mediated	Provides anonymity or high confidentiality Provides the most convenience Places the least demand on time (most efficient) Requires no data entry Minimizes errors Maximizes accuracy of responses Minimizes potential response bias Allows use of free survey software programs Can lead to larger and more diverse samples Can reach samples anywhere	Requires development of procedures to ensure that someone does not respond more than once Does not allow control over setting conditions Requires more difficult design elements (e.g., survey appearance, colors used, items per page) Excludes people without access to a reliable Internet connection Makes it easier for respondents to skip questions Requires funds to use the best survey software options Allows only low interaction with the researcher May make it difficult to get people to take the survey without an incentive

typically with statistical analysis software, to make it easier to calculate descriptive statistics (e.g., percentage of the sample in each category) and test hypotheses.

- *Ordinal* variables have an artificial range in which differences between consecutive values aren't known or equal. Survey questions might have response options measured on a Likert scale, such as one that ranges from *strongly disagree* (1) to *strongly agree* (7). On such a scale, there is no clear difference in meaning between 3 and 4, for example. In practice, we often add the responses to several ordinal questions from a single scale together and treat the total score as a scale variable.

- *Scale* variables have meaningful units and can be interval or ratio. Interval scales have values at equal intervals with no true, meaningful 0 (e.g., 0° Fahrenheit is a true temperature and does not mean there is no temperature), and ratio scales have values at equal intervals but a true 0 point (e.g., income or grade point average [GPA]). Survey questions might ask about age, height, weight, GPA, income, and so forth. We can say that someone who is 20 is half the age of someone who is 40 (i.e., being half of something carries the same meaning regardless of whether 20 is half of 40 or 100 is half of 200).

As researchers, our goal is to get the most information possible, which means we need scores that vary across people a great deal (e.g., one person scores 0, another scores 500, and many others fall somewhere in between). This is referred to as *range of variation*. To do this, we should aim to measure things at the strongest level of measurement possible—that is, scale. When this is not possible, we have two other options: nominal and ordinal. In most quantitative research, we want to explain why scores vary across people. So we need possible response options to have variation, or else we won't be able to answer our research questions. Think about this simple example of three different ways to ask a question measuring age:

1. Which best describes your age (please circle)?
   a. Young
   b. Middle-aged
   c. Old

2. Which best describes your age (please circle)?
   a. 0–12
   b. 13–17
   c. 18–25
   d. 26–55
   e. 56 or older
3. How old are you (in years)? _____

After reviewing these questions about age, you should notice that the first question is asked using a nominal level of measurement, the second using an ordinal level of measurement, and the third using a scale level of measurement. Which question do you think gives you the best, most accurate information? If you answered Question 3, you are correct! Knowing someone's exact age is better than knowing they are young or fall somewhere in the range of 18 to 25. This example provides a clear picture of the differences in quality of information obtained across the questions and of which would be most useful and have the most potential variation.

CASE STUDY: DR. HERTZOG, PART 2

Now it's time to return to the case study from Exhibit 6.1. Recall that Dr. Hertzog wants to know whether new mothers are more satisfied with life if they return to work. Read Part 2 of the Dr. Hertzog case study in Exhibit 8.1 and answer the questions. Check your answers with a colleague.

Finding Existing Measures

You might think that you have to develop all of your survey questions and measures yourself. The good thing is, you don't. People have been doing research for years and spend a good amount of time developing measures of many variables we often examine in our work. Finding them can be easier than you think. Here are a few ways to find measures:

- Mental Measurement Yearbook—Most universities have this library database, which lets you search for a measure. It provides a list of measures in the database, questions, cost, population they can be used for

Exhibit 8.1

Case Study of Dr. Hertzog, Part 2

Dr. Hertzog has decided to use the Satisfaction With Life Scale[a] to measure general life satisfaction (See Part 1 of the case study in Exhibit 6.1). The questionnaire she will give to her study participants is as follows:

*The following statements address how satisfied you are with your life. Please indicate how much you **agree** or **disagree** with each of the following statements. (Please circle your answer.)*

	Strongly disagree	Somewhat disagree	Somewhat agree	Strongly agree
1. In most ways, my life is close to my ideal.	1	2	3	4
2. The conditions of my life are excellent.	1	2	3	4
3. I am satisfied with my life.	1	2	3	4
4. So far I have gotten the important things I want in life.	1	2	3	4
5. If I could live my life over, I would change almost nothing.	1	2	3	4

1. Will this scale provide Dr. Hertzog with quantitative or qualitative data?
2. What is the level of measurement (nominal, ordinal, interval, or ratio)?
3. How would you suggest Dr. Hertzog administer this scale? Should she use a self-administered mail survey technique, telephone interviews, in-person interviews, a web survey? Why?
4. How could Dr. Hertzog triangulate her measure of general satisfaction with life?

(continues)

Exhibit 8.1
Case Study of Dr. Hertzog, Part 2 (*Continued*)
5. Dr. Hertzog decides that she also wants to conduct in-depth interviews with a subset of the participants in her study. Transform this scale into an unstructured interview guide.   *Answers:* 1. quantitative; 2. ordinal; 3. describe an administration strategy; 4. suggest a way to triangulate; 5. compose an unstructured interview guide.

[a]From "The Satisfaction With Life Scale," by E. Diener, R. A. Emmons, R. J. Larsen, and S. Griffin, 1985, *Journal of Personality Assessment, 49*, pp. 71–75. Copyright 1985 by Taylor & Francis. Adapted with permission.

(e.g., kids, adults, couples), scoring, and a lot more information. A citation also is included or information on where you can find the measure.

- Books of measures—Several books of existing measures have been published, and many libraries have copies. These books have all the same information as the database above and a copy of the measure. We find *Measures for Clinical Practice*, Volumes 1 and 2, by K. Corcoran and J. Fischer (New York, NY: Oxford University Press, 2013), to be most useful.

- Existing research—As you review previous research, take notice of what measures the authors used; if several studies used the same measure, this likely means it is a good one to use. Get the citation for the measure from the reference list and then look at that source—it likely will have a copy of the measure, or at least a list of all the questions. Or you can always email the author and ask whether he or she will share a copy. We find that researchers are willing to help out students!

- Your professor—We always have lots of measures and books of measures around our offices, probably under piles of student papers! Just ask.

Measurement Validity and Fairness

You've done the hard work of designing your study, figuring out your sampling plan, and choosing your data collection method. There's one more important thing you'll need to consider: How good are your measures? In order to interpret and be confident in your results, you need to be sure that your measure (and scores from it) actually represents what you intended to measure. To do this, you need evidence of *measurement validity*, and this often is detailed in the same place you found your measure.

Evidence can be either empirical (i.e., shown by previous research) or procedural (i.e., documented through development and administration evidence). For example, if a research study finds that a new measure of happiness is related to an existing (and demonstrated highly valid) measure of happiness, we can say there is a level of validity based on empirical evidence. However, we also would need to compare the samples and procedures of our study with those of the previous studies and to consider the conditions under which the measure was developed, who developed it, and for whom it was developed to document some level of procedural evidence. This would help demonstrate what is referred to as *relation to other measures*. Other evidence includes the following:

- *test content*—whether the items of a measure represent the range of content they should,
- *response processes* needed or used (e.g., can guessing or test-taking strategies lead to correct answers, as opposed to knowing the correct answer?),
- *internal structure*—whether the concept being measured has multiple dimensions,
- whether items show a preference for one group of respondents over another,
- how measures are scored,
- whether norms exist, and
- populations and age groups for which a measure can be used.

When considering, and documenting, these types of evidence, you also should be mindful of documenting issues of fairness. Fairness is related to use of measures with intended populations (e.g., if a measure was meant to be used with adults, you shouldn't use it with children) but also includes a commitment to ensuring that your measures accurately demonstrate people's abilities, knowledge, emotions, thoughts, and so forth. To ensure accuracy, you must include items or questions that are readable, clear, concise, and nonbiased and that are presented in a way that is accessible and sensitive. Suppose you developed a survey using your measure of happiness and decided to make it visually appealing by using red instead of black ink. How accessible would this be to people who have red–green color blindness? Their score might be 0 because they did not see any questions and skipped them all. This would not accurately represent their happiness. The main takeaway is that when you use a preexisting measure, look for information about whom it should be used with and under what conditions and how it should be scored, and report it all in your proposal.

Measurement Reliability

Measurement reliability refers to the extent to which a measure can consistently and reliably measure the target construct, and do so with precision. There are four different ways to assess measurement reliability: (a) test–retest reliability, (b) interitem reliability, (c) alternate-forms reliability, and (d) interrater reliability. We will discuss *interrater reliability*, or the agreement between two or more people coding the same behavior, in the section on observation later in this chapter.

Test–retest reliability means that when you measure the same construct at two different points in time, you get essentially the same results. Keep in mind that when establishing test–retest reliability, you should make sure no intervention occurs between the measurement time points that might lead to a difference in scores on the measure. You need to establish that your measure has test–retest reliability before you use it in your study.

Interitem reliability refers to the extent to which a set of items in a measure are correlated or hang together. For example, if you have a scale that measures self-esteem and consists of five separate items, you should ensure that those five items are highly correlated with one another. This correlation is typically reported in research articles using Cronbach's alpha, which is the most commonly reported type of measurement reliability.

Alternate-forms reliability is the extent to which slightly different versions of the same measure are highly correlated. You probably took the SAT. Nowadays, the SAT is offered as a computerized test, but when we took the SATs, the only option was a paper-based form. When the Educational

Testing Service was developing the electronic SAT, they assessed alternate-forms reliability by asking a sample of people who had taken the paper-based SAT to also take the computerized version. One of us, Jen, was one of those test takers, and she is pleased to report that she got the exact same score on the paper-based version and the computerized version, thereby demonstrating alternate-forms reliability.

Developing Survey Questions

Sometimes you need to write your own questions to measure one or more of your variables of interest. This is typically the case when you are measuring demographic questions, when you are measuring a newer variable that hasn't been studied before, when the measure you want costs money, or when the measures you find are too long and you are concerned about keeping your survey short for participants. Writing a good question that measures what it is supposed to (see the section on validity above) is harder than you may imagine. Just ask any professor who has written an exam, or think about some of the questions on an exam you have taken.

As a general rule, pilot test your questions with a few friends or, even better, a few people who would be likely respondents (Don't forget to include a formal pilot test in your institutional review board [IRB] proposal). Questions should be clear, simple, direct, and written at about a seventh- or eighth-grade reading level for adults and age appropriate for children. A student once shared with us that she had her younger brother read the questions, and he was able to really help her word things at a correct reading level using clear language. It was a great tip, and we highly recommend doing it. If you don't have a younger sibling, simply ask around, and we bet someone will help you out. If you use Microsoft Word, you also can run the readability statistics, and they will tell you the reading level of a sentence, an entire survey, or a paper for a class. Three additional guidelines for writing questions are as follows:

1. For a set of questions that all measure the same variable, it can be good to mix the direction of the wording to monitor for *response bias*, or

the likelihood that a respondent will answer all questions in the same way or by always selecting the same option (this assumes the use of response options on a Likert scale).

a. Being part of the learning community prepared me for graduate school.

b. Taking part in research projects as part of the learning community did not prepare me for graduate school.

2. Avoid *double-barreled questions,* which embed multiple questions in a single item. In the example below, the question asks about two different concepts: studying and learning. If a person enjoys learning but not studying, how would they answer?

a. To what extent do you like studying and learning chemistry?

A better option:

a. To what extent do you like learning chemistry?

b. To what extent do you like studying chemistry?

3. Avoid leading or loaded questions. *Leading questions* do what you would expect: They lead respondents to answer in a particular way. *Loaded questions* do something similar but rely on introducing bias to lead respondents into answering in a particular way.

Leading version of the question:

a. Do you agree ["do you agree" implies that respondents should agree with you] that students in the learning community should be expected to study?

Loaded versions of the question:

a. Students in the learning community should be expected to study. Do you believe the same? [a value statement is made and then the question is asked]

b. Most professors in the learning community ["most" introduces bias because it suggests that a majority of people and people in a position of authority believe something] believe that students should study. Do you believe the same?

A better option:

a. To what extent do you believe students in the learning community should be expected to study?

Now that you have some direction for writing questions, we also need to talk about selecting response options. Again, most questions you write to study variables likely will use Likert scales as the response options (see Exhibit 8.2). Most people understand a response range from *strongly agree* (1) to *strongly disagree* (7), but there are several considerations that make this a more difficult decision. Let's take a look at several option types.

The first three scales in Exhibit 8.2 all share a range of seven options participants could select. Because it is important to obtain variation in our scores, the use of seven options is a good choice compared with three or even five. But there are two other considerations.

First, because you include an odd number of options, respondents can effectively choose the middle ground (i.e., a neutral response, or 4). An odd number of options is not always a good choice depending on the variable being measured. You should ask yourself whether a neutral option makes

Exhibit 8.2

Examples of Likert Scale Presentation

Strongly agree						Strongly disagree
1	2	3	4	5	6	7

Strongly agree			Neither agree nor disagree			Strongly disagree
1	2	3	4	5	6	7

Strongly agree	Agree	Agree a little	Neither agree nor disagree	Disagree a little	Disagree	Strongly disagree
1	2	3	4	5	6	7

Strongly agree	Agree	Agree a little	Disagree a little	Disagree	Strongly disagree
1	2	3	4	5	6

sense or not. If you are really interested in people making a definitive choice (i.e., "forced choice") about what you are asking, you need to use an equal number of response options. We suggest using six, as seen in the fourth scale of Exhibit 8.2.

The second consideration is the use of anchors, which define in words the number options. Looking at the first scale in the exhibit, if we asked you what a 2 meant compared to a 3, could you tell us? We are sure you could give us an answer. However, the likelihood of a 2 meaning the same thing to you as it does to everyone else answering this question is a big assumption to make, and not a good one. This potential inconsistency is one of the main issues with using an ordinal level of measurement. To promote consistent use of responses, use anchors (e.g., agree, disagree) to give respondents a frame of reference. Anchors make it a little more likely that when two people select 6, their responses will be comparable. There are two ways to go about this. The second scale provides anchors on each endpoint and one in the middle. The third scale provides an anchor word for each of the seven response options. In most cases, the third scale is the best to use. The same would hold for Likert questions using equal options, such as the fourth scale.

The final major consideration for response options is ensuring the options are mutually exclusive and exhaustive. Stated more simply, every-one should be able to pick one and only one option. Let's return to our previous ordinal level example for age. Exhibit 8.3 shows three examples, and only one is mutually exclusive and exhaustive. Take a look and see if you can figure out why.

Exhibit 8.3
Which Choice Is Mutually Exclusive and Exhaustive?

Response option	Choice 1	Choice 2	Choice 3
1	0–12	0–12	0–12
2	13–18	12–18	13–18
3	19–33	18–33	19–33
4	34–60	33–60+	34–60+
	Not exhaustive	Not exclusive	Exhaustive and exclusive

For Choice 1, you should notice that it is not exhaustive because there is no response choice for anyone over the age of 60. Choice 2 is not exclusive because people who are 18 could pick Option 2 or 3. Choice 3 allows people of any age to pick one and only one option. This might seem fairly simple, but you would be surprised at how many researchers, novice and seasoned, make this error.

The last thing you should know about surveys is how to make them appear professional and pleasing to the eye. You also want them to be easy to follow. There is a lot of research about formatting and ordering tasks, and newer research has begun to identify unique formatting considerations for online surveys as well. For example, research shows that asking participants to report on demographics at the beginning of a survey can influence the way they answer the remaining questions. This is known as the *stereotype threat*. Asking participants to report their gender at the beginning of a survey measuring math skills may prime girls to subconsciously think about the stereotype that girls are not as good at math as boys and therefore may result in poorer performance on the math questions.

Pointers for General Surveys

Here are a few pointers for general surveys:

1. Do not begin with demographic questions because this can introduce response bias.
2. Begin with nonsensitive questions. This helps ease people into the survey and makes them more comfortable answering questions. What would it be like if someone you didn't know walked up to you and asked you when was the last time you hooked up, before even asking your name and introducing himself or herself?
3. Number the questions. We find it helpful to separate a survey into sections with short titles that give the respondent a sense of the questions about to be asked of them; for example, see Exhibit 8.4. If you use this approach, there is another benefit. For each new section, you can begin the number of questions with the number 1 each time so the number of questions seems smaller than the actual

---

Exhibit 8.4

Survey Structure With Section Headings and Questions Numbered for Each Section for a Study on Experiences in a Learning Community

About your research experiences in the learning community:

1. Question 1
2. Question 2

A little about you:

1. Demographic question
2. Demographic question

---

number. In the example in Exhibit 8.4, the largest number a respondent would see is 2, even though there are 4 questions. Psychologically, this helps respondents perceive the survey to be shorter, thereby reducing the likelihood of fatigue, frustration ("When will this survey end?!"), and dropout.

4. Help respondents find their answer choice easily to reduce error. Exhibits 8.5 and 8.6 show two ways to do this: dots and matrixes. Dots (Exhibit 8.5) lead the eye to the correct number to circle. Matrixes (Exhibit 8.6) help people remember and locate response options and anchors. Be careful not to use too many questions within one matrix, and don't let a matrix go over continuously to the next page. Also, to help reduce error, it is helpful to shade every other line.

Exhibit 8.5

Use of Dots to Lead the Eye to the Correct Response

Which best represents your age? *(Circle one.)*

0–12 1
13–18 2
19–25 3

Exhibit 8.6

Example of a Response Matrix

	Strongly agree	Agree	Agree a little	Disagree a little	Disagree	Strongly disagree
Question 1	1	2	3	4	5	6
Question 2	1	2	3	4	5	6
Question 3	1	2	3	4	5	6

Special Considerations for Online Surveys

Most people complete an online survey quicker than the same survey in paper form. However, online participants are more sensitive to time in that they expect online surveys to take less time to complete than in-person surveys. To help with this, we suggest using a progress bar. The progress bar should be placed at the bottom right of the page so it is the last thing a respondent sees before clicking on the *next* button to go on to the next page of questions. Seeing that they are making progress makes it more likely they will click to the next page rather than click out of the survey.

A related consideration is to manage the number of questions on any one page. In other words, do not put all your questions on one page. Instead, consider doing one page for each variable you measure and then one page for your demographic questions. Because the length of measures varies, another guideline is to include about 10 to 15 questions per page.

The final suggestion is related to color. Online survey tools have so many color options it is easy to create a rainbow survey. Resist this temptation: It is extremely distracting to research participants! It also is helpful to remember that some people are color-blind. At the same time, a stark white screen can hurt the eyes, especially the longer people stare at it. We suggest using soft shades of grey—one for the main background of each page and one slightly darker for use in the matrix questions. You are now a few steps closer to being a survey expert!

OBSERVATION

Observation, in which the researcher directly observes people's behaviors, can be an excellent data collection technique. One of the primary benefits of observational techniques is that they can be conducted in the field, where you can learn about how the context may influence behavior. It is also a useful technique when you are interested in studying a population that cannot respond to questionnaires or interviews (e.g., young children). The disadvantages of using observational techniques are that you can observe only small groups at once and that it can be a fairly labor-intensive process.

Types of Observation

There are several different types of observation, and your choice will largely depend on your research question and the specific population you are studying. When acting as a *covert observer*, the researcher does not identify himself or herself as a researcher and observes without actually participating with the group. This approach is typically used in a public place where people watching wouldn't seem odd. When acting as a *complete observer*, the researcher publicly identifies himself or herself as a researcher and observes without participating with the group. This approach is often used when conducting classroom observations. When acting as a *covert participant*, the researcher does not identify himself or herself as a researcher and observes while participating with the group. This approach raises the most ethical concerns. Finally, when acting as a *participant observer*, the researcher identifies himself or herself as a researcher and observes while participating with the group. This approach is often associated with ethnographic research.

Before selecting an observation technique, it is important to consider how your presence as a researcher might affect the actions of others. As you might expect, an individual or group might change their behavior if they know they are being observed; this is referred to as *reactive effects*.

Conducting Observations

When conducting observations, it is important to take careful notes, which can take several different forms. *Jottings* are brief notes that are usually written while observing. *Field notes* are usually written after an observation session and describe what was seen or heard.

Coding sheets are a more formalized way of systematically documenting what was observed. Systematic observation is particularly useful when more than one observer is conducting observations. A coding sheet is a standard form that multiple observers use to record what they see and hear. These records can then be used to establish *interrater reliability*, or the extent to which two or more observers rating the same person or event agree with one another. Interrater is one form of measurement reliability; additional types of measurement reliability were discussed earlier in this chapter. If multiple observers use the same coding sheet to rate the same thing and get similar results, you can be more confident that the ratings accurately reflect what was being observed. You are most likely to get good interrater reliability when the instructions for coding are clear. Exhibit 8.7 shows a coding sheet that was used to code Super Bowl commercials.

Now it's your turn to try and develop a coding sheet. Complete the activity in Exhibit 8.8. Once you have developed your coding sheet, try it out. Find a friend, and both of you observe the same event together. Each of you should fill out the coding sheet. Compare your observations. What proportion of agreement did you have? You can calculate interrater reliability by dividing the total number of agreed-on items by the total number of items coded and multiplying by 100.

Exhibit 8.7

Code Sheet for Television Advertisements

Product being advertised: _____

Number of people appearing in commercial: ☐ 1 ☐ 2 ☐ 3 ☐ 4

Location: ☐ Domestic ☐ Public

Attributes of principal actor:

    Gender: ☐ Male ☐ Female

    Apparent age: ☐ Baby ☐ Child ☐ Teen
                   ☐ Young adult ☐ Adult ☐ Older adult

Exhibit 8.8

Developing a Coding Sheet Activity

You have noticed that many preschool classrooms have several activity areas, such as blocks, a doll corner, reading nook, and others. You have also noticed that during free play, boys and girls seem to have different preferences for activities. You are interested in conducting a study looking at whether the activity preferences of preschool children differ by sex. You decide to conduct an observational study at the local preschool. In order to record your observations, you decide to use a coding sheet. Design a coding sheet that could be used to record your preschool classroom observations.

IN-DEPTH INTERVIEWS

There are three main types of interview: structured, unstructured, and semistructured. *Structured interviews* are those in which participants are asked all of the exact same questions and the questions do not change in subsequent interviews. *Unstructured interviews* are those in which no, or almost no, questions are planned in advance. These interviews are most often used in ethnography, when you don't know what questions to ask until you are immersed in the culture being studied.

Semistructured interviews are the most common. This type of interview contains a set of basic questions that are asked of all participants, but, depending on what participants share, you might develop new questions on the spot as a way to explore something they said with more depth or because they shared something you had not considered when developing your questions and you want to know more. The new questions might become part of your interview guide for all new participants, or they might be specific to that one interview. This strategy provides you with flexibility to follow participants and what they have to share and is another way in which qualitative research is emergent.

A good interview guide has two overarching types of question: main and prompt. The main questions are broader and are planned to help you answer your research questions. Prompts are used to help make sure you get the information you need and to allow you to dig deeper into someone's experience or story. Qualitative interview questions are among the most interesting and most difficult to write. Like survey questions, interview questions should be written at an appropriate reading level, nonleading, nonjudgmental, and asked one at a time. It is easy to ask multiple questions at once without realizing it, and this should be avoided. There needs to be a good balance between broadness and specificity as well.

Above all else, interview questions must be open-ended, and we find this to be the most challenging part about writing them. So let's start there first. A closed-ended question can be answered with one or two words. For example, "Do you like to study?" can be answered with a yes or no. An open-ended question requires the participant to provide explanation and details. For example, "How do you study?" requires more than a simple yes or no. However, that question is too broad. Studying for an exam might be different from studying for a quiz or from general studying when preparing for class when a new topic is going to be discussed. A better option might be "How do you prepare for an exam?" This question is open-ended (*how do you*), general (*prepare for*), and specific (*an exam*). Of course, it does assume the participant prepares for her or his exam, but *prepare* might be a better, less assumptive word choice than *study*.

Let's return to the idea of using prompt questions to gain more depth. After reviewing the literature on how students prepare for exams, you find out that the most common strategies include reading and reviewing notes and PowerPoint slides, and some people study alone, whereas others study in groups. Because these strategies are described in the previous literature, you know it likely is important to get information about each of these during the interview. To help, you should develop prompt questions for each. The participant might naturally discuss each of these without you needing to use a prompt question—this is a sign that you wrote a super main question! For our purposes, let's suppose you need them.

The overall purpose of your study was to understand the process college students use to prepare for an exam. After asking the main question, your participant shared that she rereads all the chapters for the exam twice. Certainly this is helpful information, but it lacks depth. For example, does she skim the pages, read each word, take notes while reading, highlight important phrases, focus only on definitions, think about ways to apply what she is reading to different real life scenarios, or do something else? There is a lot of depth to be gained here. You could use several prompt questions to help you understand more about her reading process. Here are a few examples:

- "You mentioned that you reread all the chapters that will be on the exam. Can you tell me a little more about how you determine what information you are reading is important to remember for the exam?"
- "I noticed you have a textbook with you. It would help me understand more if you read a page from one of the chapters and walk me through how you think about the material as you are reading it."
- "If I opened one of your textbooks and looked at a chapter you read when preparing for an exam, what would it look like? For example, some people might highlight words or write notes in the margin, or even doodle." *Subprompt*: "How did you decide to highlight that specific sentence?"

Prompt questions can help you gain a deeper understanding of the topic you are researching. We also should mention that *how* questions are among the best to use. Contrary to what you might think, the use of *why* questions is not as effective for qualitative interviews. Avoid closed-ended questions followed by a tag-on *why*: for example, "Do you like studying? Why or why not?"

Aside from questions used to gather demographic information, there are a few types of specific question you might find useful when developing an interview guide. In life, most of our experiences have emotional, cognitive, behavioral, and sensory components to them. When you want to gain depth of understanding about someone's experience, you should ask questions that explore each of these components. You also might want to ask about facts and opinions or values. Using the preparing for an exam example above, the following are questions representing each specific type:

- Factual—"How much time do you spend preparing when you have an exam?"
- Opinion—"What is your opinion about preparing for exams?"
- Value—"Can you share with me what value you believe preparing for exams might have?"
- Emotional—"How do you feel while you are preparing for an exam?"
- Cognitive—"When rereading chapters in preparation for an exam, how do you think about what you are reading?"
- Behavioral—"Can you tell me about a typical time you prepared for an exam?"
- Sensory—"What kinds of sounds might be around you while you are preparing for an exam?"

Two additional categories you might find helpful include devil's advocate and hypothetical questions. These questions often help you understand some of the components of experience listed above but are more interesting questions to ask:

- Devil's advocate—"Some people might say that preparing for an exam is pointless. How would you respond to them?"
- Hypothetical—"Pretend that you have an exam tomorrow. How would you prepare?"

Although there are many options for types of questions, it is best to plan for three or four main questions and rely more on prompts.

Now you can write great interview questions and are almost ready to start collecting interview data, or at least to submit an IRB application. At this point, it is good to put your questions and interview plan on paper in a more formal way: This is referred to as your *interview protocol*. The protocol helps you remember each part of the process, including what questions you plan to ask, and also is a good way to structure notes and documentation. There are four main parts of the protocol—(a) basic information, (b) data collection, (c) interview guide, and (d) ending instructions—and an outline is included in Exhibit 8.9 for you to use.

FOCUS GROUPS

Although you likely will not attempt a focus group as part of your first research project, they are really fun and interesting, so we wanted to share a few quick tips to help you see the potential of using this data collection method. Focus groups are like interviewing a bunch of people at once, but they are different in that you focus more on the interactions between group members. You may be familiar with the saying "The whole is greater than the sum of its parts." This captures the uniqueness of focus groups well. What you get from a focus group is all the individual interview responses, but you also get a great deal more information.

Exhibit 8.9
Interview Protocol Outline
Name of Study
Basic Information
Date:
Time:
Interviewer:
Interviewee:
Location of the interview: [Add notes about the setting, e.g., "Interviewer and interviewee were sitting next to each other on a couch, the TV was on, and children were playing in the background."]
Data Collection
■ Turn on the voice recorder (we suggest using two in case one fails).
■ Introduce yourself.

Exhibit 8.9

Interview Protocol Outline (*Continued*)

- Engage in rapport building.
- Explain the purpose of the study.
- Discuss how the interview will work.
- Go over informed consent.
- Ask if there are any questions.
- Obtain the signed consent form.

Interview Guide

Question 1

Prompt 1

Prompt 2

(Leave space for notes here, and don't forget to document any nonverbal behaviors that might be important.)

Question 2

Prompt 1

Prompt 2

Ending Instructions

- Thank the interviewee and provide the incentive (if applicable).
- Remind the interviewee of confidentiality.
- Provide the interviewee with details about when you expect further contact (e.g., to share findings).
- Provide your contact information.
- Ask if the interviewee has any questions.
- Thank the interviewee for participating again.
- Exit the interview location.

Think about one of the best class discussions you have been a part of in which many members of the class shared their experiences, as opposed to a class where only one or two people spoke most of the time. You probably learned a lot more when the majority participated; it was more fun, and hearing other peoples' experiences likely made you think of something you hadn't before or in a way you had never considered. That is exactly the type of unique information you seek to gain when using a focus group. You want people to bounce off each other's ideas and react to each other's thoughts and stories.

You also probably have had different experiences with this in classes of different sizes. If the class is too small, fewer ideas are generated. If it is too large, there is less discussion and fewer people willing to talk. The same is true in focus groups and is another Goldilocks problem (see Chapter 2). An ideal in-person focus group size is about eight, although a couple of people won't show up, so you might want to schedule 10. In an online focus group, things move a bit faster, so it is best to keep the size a little smaller, around four or five.

In a class, the first day usually involves some type of icebreaker or introductions. This is good practice for focus groups as well. You might want to allow people a few minutes to simply chat with each other and even provide snacks. Participants will naturally chat while getting food. You also should develop a question that allows people to introduce and share a little about themselves. The guidelines for developing good questions are similar to those for an in-depth interview. The main difference is the use of prompts: Not only do you need good prompts, but you also need to use prompts that encourage interaction. Examples include the following:

- "Harvey, what did hearing about Joan's experience preparing for an exam make you think?"
- "How about everyone else; what did you all think when hearing about Joan's experience?"
- "Markus, we haven't heard from you yet. I am curious what you think as you're hearing everyone else."
- "Joan, what is it like hearing everyone's reaction to your exam preparations?"

As you might see, your role is to facilitate interaction among members even more than to ask lots of interview questions. If you spend a good amount of time creating rapport at the beginning, you likely won't even need to facilitate interaction; it will simply happen. That's an indicator that you are now a rock star researcher!

CASE STUDY: DR. HERTZOG, PARTS 3 AND 4

Now it's time to return to the case study of Dr. Hertzog. Read Exhibits 8.10 and 8.11 and answer the questions. Check your answers with a colleague.

APPLYING CONCEPTS TO YOUR RESEARCH PROPOSAL

Now you're ready to write the Measures section of your proposal. Briefly describe, in one or two sentences, each of the variables you are interested in measuring. For each variable, write a paragraph in which you describe how you will measure the variable. Remember that you do not need to reinvent the wheel and come up with a new measure. Begin by doing a search in the literature for tools that have already been created to measure the variable in which you are interested. If you cannot locate a measure in the literature, you may need to begin thinking about developing your own measure.

Whether you find an already existing measure or create your own, try to be specific in describing it. If you plan on using a questionnaire, how many items will there be? What are some example questions? Will it be administered in person, by phone, or online? If you are using observation, will you use a coding sheet or checklist? What exactly will you include in the coding sheet? Sample measures should be included in the appendix of the research proposal. For each variable, describe in one or two sentences how you will determine that the measure is reliable and valid. Now reread your proposal draft, especially the Design section, and revise it as needed to reflect the measures you've chosen.

Exhibit 8.10

Case Study of Dr. Hertzog, Part 3

Dr. Hertzog decides to use a quasi-experimental design (see Part 1 in Exhibit 6.1 and Part 2 in Exhibit 8.1). Specifically, she decides to use the nonequivalent groups design. She also decides to use a longitudinal approach. She plans on recruiting working women who are pregnant for the first time to participate in her study. She has contacted local obstetricians and gotten them to agree to hand out information about her study to their patients. The information sheet includes a brief description of the study and asks the women to fill out a short questionnaire and return it to Dr. Hertzog along with a consent form. The questionnaire asks several questions about the women's age, current work status, and intention to work after the birth of their baby.

Dr. Hertzog decides to use a quota sampling strategy. She wants to be sure that her sample includes both women who intend to return to work and those who do not. She knows that she wants the total sample size to include 200 women. She has decided to include in her study the first 120 women who indicate that they intend to return to work and the first 120 women who indicate that they do not intend to return to work.

After determining who will be in her study, she plans on asking all of the women to complete a measure of general life satisfaction. This measure will be completed while the women are still pregnant and working. Six months after the women have given birth, Dr. Hertzog plans on contacting them again. At this point she will ask them whether they have returned to work, and she will also ask them to complete the same measure on general life satisfaction again.

Dr. Hertzog is interested in using a mixed-methods approach; that is, she would like to collect both quantitative and qualitative data. She believes that the quantitative data will give her the information she needs to understand whether women who do not return

Exhibit 8.10

Case Study of Dr. Hertzog, Part 3 (*Continued*)

to work after the birth of a child are indeed more satisfied with life. However, she also wants to understand why women are more or less satisfied with life after the birth of a child. She has therefore decided to also include a qualitative data component.

1. Draw a visual representation of the design that Dr. Hertzog has elected to use.
2. If Dr. Hertzog wanted only 200 women in her final sample, why did she recruit 240 women?
3. Dr. Hertzog wants to use both a quantitative and a qualitative approach in her study. How would you suggest she collect quantitative data? How would you suggest she collect qualitative data? In other words, what data collection methods should she use?
4. What type of sampling technique would you suggest Dr. Hertzog use to obtain a sample?
5. How would you suggest Dr. Hertzog recruit participants for her study?

Answers: 1. pretest → return to work → posttest, pretest → don't return to work → posttest; 2. she wants to oversample in case there is attrition (i.e., participants drop out of the study before it is completed); 3. describe appropriate data collection methods; 4. suggest a sampling technique; 5. suggest a recruiting technique.

Exhibit 8.11

Case Study of Dr. Hertzog, Part 4

Dr. Hertzog is concerned that there are possible extraneous variables that could potentially affect a woman's general life satisfaction after the birth of a baby other than just whether or not she returns to work (See Part 1 in Exhibit 6.1, Part 2 in Exhibit 8.1, and Part 3 in Exhibit 8.10). She hypothesizes that one plausible alternative explanation (or extraneous variable) is partner support. In order to test this alternative explanation, she decides to ask the women in her study to complete a questionnaire that asks about how supportive their partner is. She searches the research literature and is unable to locate a survey instrument that measures partner support. She decides that she will need to construct her own measure.

1. Dr. Hertzog has asked for your help in designing a short survey instrument that will measure partner support in a relationship. Design a survey instrument that Dr. Hertzog can use in her study.
2. How will you assess the validity of your measure?
3. How will you assess the reliability of your measure?

Answers: 1. design a survey; 2. describe a means of assessing validity; 3. describe a means of assessing reliability.

9

Establishing Validity
for Quantitative Studies

You'll be investing a lot of time in the research you do, especially before you even begin to collect data. It makes sense, then, that you want your research to produce the most accurate results possible. Who wants to waste their time or fail a class, right? Often, when you talk about the accuracy of your results in a quantitative study, you are referring to your ability to demonstrate cause and effect between at least two variables—this is called *internal validity.* Even more so, you hope your results can be generalized to describe contexts and/or populations outside of your sample—this is called *external validity.* There are many threats to internal and external validity. Some of these you can plan for by including certain research design elements, and others pop up during the process as "uh-oh" moments. This chapter discusses ways to establish validity in quantitative research studies, with a slightly larger focus on internal validity.

Most threats to validity relate to experimental designs because those designs are the primary ones that can determine cause and effect (some

http://dx.doi.org/10.1037/0000049-009
Designing and Proposing Your Research Project, by J. B. Urban and B. M. van Eeden-Moorefield

longitudinal designs can, as well). However, that does not mean there is no use for validity in nonexperimental studies. In fact, we believe there are several applications of validity important to nonexperimental research, including qualitative studies.

HISTORY THREAT

For example, one type of threat to validity is history. *History* refers to the ability of an event that occurs just before or during data collection in a study to potentially influence the results. Let's take the U.S. Supreme Court's decision to legalize marriage for same-sex couples. Suppose you were collecting data for a study examining the role of social support from family, friends, and society for all couples in romantic relationships, regardless of sexual orientation, and you were collecting data from March to September 2015 (the decision was announced June 2015):

- Do you believe this decision might have influenced the way any of these couples thought about social support?
- Do you think participants who completed your study in March would be differentially influenced by the announcement of the decision compared with those who participated in August?
- Do you think this decision would influence the results of your study?

If you answered yes to any of these questions, then you likely have a history threat, and we would agree. It completely makes sense (and research supports) that most same-sex couples would feel more socially supported after the Supreme Court's decision that legitimized their relationships. So, responses to questions about social support in your study would vary by when people participated (before or after the decision). We also could argue that most (not all) different-sex couples should not be affected much, or in the same ways, because this decision had nothing to do with the ability of their relationships to be supported or recognized. This means that the results you get might reflect responses to the court's decision more than typical responses in the absence of a court decision, and this would likely be the case for one group more than the other. The takeaway here is that the validity of your results just decreased because of an event in history.

Now, do you think the history threat influence on your results would be different if you designed an experimental versus a nonexperimental study? This could go either way. If you were conducting a nonexperimental study, there is basically one way to determine the extent of any possible history effects: You could create a new variable that indicated whether someone participated before or after the court decision, and then you could statistically control for it. A bit crude, but it works fairly well. If you used an experimental design with random assignment, then you could assume that the sexual orientation of participants and the variety of ways in which all participants would be influenced were equivalent across groups. This design partially takes care of the history threat in that it evens it out for you. However, the results would still contain the threat in a way that you cannot easily tease out. For both cases, the best thing to do is talk about the court decision and its potential impact on the results in the Discussion section and report it as a limitation to the study.

Remember, no study is perfect, so having limitations is generally not a big deal. Table 9.1 summarizes the main types of threats to internal and external validity, including a description of each threat and several considerations you can make to address the threat when designing your study or when analyzing the results of your study.

APPLYING CONCEPTS TO YOUR RESEARCH PROPOSAL

Exhibit 9.1 is a worksheet you can use when planning your study to determine whether any unplanned threats occurred during data collection. The worksheet includes spaces for you to identify which threats to validity might be most relevant to your study, explain why you think so (this will be great to use when you write your proposal or have to field a question from your professor), identify other studies that addressed the same type of validity threat you expect (you can use these citations in your Method section), explain how these other studies addressed the threat, and describe a plan to limit the threat. Now reread your research proposal, especially the Design section, and revise it as needed to reflect your plans for maximizing validity.

Table 9.1

Validity Threats and Design Considerations to Control Them

Type	Description	Design considerations
Internal validity threats	Threats to the accuracy of a cause–effect relationship	
History	When an event happens shortly before or during the study that could influence participants' responses to surveys or behavior during a study	Statistically control for the history influence if there are multiple groups in the study and not all experienced the same event.
		Explore in the Discussion section how the event might have influenced the results.
Maturation	When people change, grow, or develop over the course of a study in ways that might influence results. This change could be short term, such as fatigue because the survey is too long, or long term, such as cognitive development when a study takes multiple years to complete.	Minimize the time it takes to complete a single session during a study.
		Include only relevant questions on surveys to minimize survey size.
		Collect data during times of the day when people are less likely to be hungry or tired.
		For longitudinal studies, measure relevant types of maturation so they can be statistically controlled.
Testing	When the same measure is used multiple times (e.g., pretest and posttest), making it possible that participants will become sensitized and used to it. Essentially, taking the measure once can influence how participants take it a second time. For some types of measure (e.g., achievement), multiple administrations of the same test act as practice tests.	Use different measures or items for each administration (make sure they all have good measurement validity and reliability).
		Increase time between testing events.

Table 9.1 ·

Validity Threats and Design Considerations to Control Them (*Continued*)

Type	Description	Design considerations
Selection or selection bias	When there are differences between groups (e.g., one has a higher average IQ) that might influence results, or when people with certain characteristics are more likely to participate in the study	Create group equivalency. Use random assignment or matching. Add questions that allow you to test for group differences and then control for them.
Instrumentation	When measurements do not work equally well each time they are used	Select measures carefully. Test physical measurement devices (e.g., stopwatch, scales) consistently over the course of a study. Use the same measures at each administration.
Mortality	When people drop out of a study (e.g., are no longer willing to participate, move away, die). Dropout is especially problematic when many people drop out and when dropout rates are different between groups.	Statistically test for differences between participants who dropped out and stayed in, and control for any differences that are present. Offer incentives to stay in the study. Gather multiple contact methods (e.g., phone, email, mailing address) from participants. Obtain a larger sample than needed to allow for potential dropout.
Statistical regression	When people with extreme scores tend to regress to the mean with subsequent administrations of a test rather than because of an experimental manipulation	Select highly reliable measures. Look for outliers in the data, and consider whether removing them from the data set is justified. Screen for people with extreme scores, and exclude them from participating.

(continues)

Table 9.1

Validity Threats and Design Considerations to Control Them (*Continued*)

Type	Description	Design considerations
Diffusion of treatment	When participants in control and experimental groups compare their experiences with each other during the study	Attempt to keep groups apart during the study, or obtain your sample from different locations.
Demoralization	When a control group feels deprived if they realize they are not receiving the experimental stimulus or intervention	Use a placebo so groups will not know who is in the experimental and control groups. Try to provide something beneficial to both groups.
Compensatory rivalry	When members of a control group realize they are not in the experimental group and try harder rather than feel deprived and give up (almost the opposite of demoralization)	Try to provide something beneficial to both groups. Use a wait-list control group (i.e., a group that receives the experimental condition after the rest of the experiment is complete) rather than a no-treatment control group.
Time order	When it cannot be determined whether the independent variable precedes the dependent variable in time	Gather data at multiple time points.
Researcher effects	When the researcher treats a group differently	Use a double-blind design in which the data collector does not know who is in the control and experimental groups.
Participant effects	When participants act differently because they know they are part of a study	Use a social desirability scale. Obtain good baseline data.
External validity threats	Threats to the generalizability of findings	
Ecological validity	When people act different in a lab setting compared with the settings of their everyday life	Conduct research with people in their own environments (often entails a loss of control over other potential threats). Use warm-up tasks to provide participants time to become comfortable.

Table 9.1

Validity Threats and Design Considerations to Control Them (*Continued*)

Type	Description	Design considerations
Selection–treatment interactions	When participant characteristics and demographics are limited, limiting the ability to generalize	Use a more generalizable sampling frame with probability sampling. Report the limitation, and do not attempt to overgeneralize the results.
History–treatment interactions	When results of studies are limited to the time period in which the study occurred	Do not attempt to generalize to other time periods. Use replication designs covering additional time periods.

Exhibit 9.1

Worksheet for Planning and Tracking Validity in My Study

Type of validity threat	Rationale	Example citation	How they did it	My plans for design considerations
List name of threat.	Explain why or how this might be a threat to your study (e.g., history).	Cite studies from the research that experienced or controlled for a similar threat.	Explain what procedures the study authors used to control for this validity threat.	Explain your plans to control this threat in the design of your study.

10

Establishing Validity for Qualitative Studies

As you read in Chapter 9, there are several types of quantitative experimental validity and strategies to help ensure we reasonably obtain it in our research. In qualitative research, researchers also are concerned with issues of validity, but there are some key differences. We should state from the beginning that validity terminology varies widely among qualitative researchers and that the terms we use reflect our preferences and theoretical orientations. From this point forward, we refer to qualitative validity as *trustworthiness*, or the extent to which findings can be trusted as accurate representations of the data and the lives, cultures, and contexts from which they come.

Let's pretend that someone you interviewed for a research study on favorite colors told you her favorite color was apple red. At the end of the study, your findings state that the participant's favorite color is red. In this instance, your study would lack a level of trustworthiness. There are many nuanced shades of red, so stating your participant likes *red* rather than

http://dx.doi.org/10.1037/0000049-010
Designing and Proposing Your Research Project, by J. B. Urban and B. M. van Eeden-Moorefield

apple red is a surface-level finding that does not capture the participant's color preference with high accuracy. For qualitative research to be trustworthy, you must capture the nuances, and do so with accuracy.

TYPES OF TRUSTWORTHINESS

There are several types of trustworthiness and many strategies to use to help ensure and demonstrate it. Table 10.1 lists and describes the main types. Importantly, it includes a column of key questions that researchers

Table 10.1
Types of Trustworthiness, Definitions, and Key Questions Addressed

Type	Definition	Key questions to ask yourself
General trustworthiness	Extent to which the research process and its findings can be trusted as accurate	How thorough was I during the entire research process? How can I be relatively certain I uncovered everything about the topic I studied?
Credibility	Extent to which findings represent the reality of participants' experiences and perceptions	Do the findings represent the lives of participants, and not my beliefs about them and their experiences? Do the findings represent the lives and experiences of participants, or did I allow previous research and theory to inform my interpretation of participants' stories? Did I use enough prompt questions to explore all potential multiple realities or varied experiences of participants?
Transferability	Extent to which findings from one study can apply to other populations, situations, or contexts	Have I provided enough information to ensure that outsiders fully understand how the findings emerged, especially information related to the sample, the contexts in which they live, and the settings where data were collected?

	Table 10.1	
Types of Trustworthiness, Definitions,		
and Key Questions Addressed (*Continued*)		
Type	Definition	Key questions to ask yourself
Dependability	Extent of consistency related to the findings	How am I going to include an outsider perspective in the research process?
		Would others agree that the findings make sense, even if they don't necessarily agree with them?
		Have I provided enough information to ensure that outsiders fully understand how the findings emerged?
Confirmability	Extent to which the researcher was aware of, monitored, and ensured that biases did not influence the research process and findings	What do I believe about the topic?
		What are the areas of similarity and difference between my beliefs about the topic and my research findings?
		How might my beliefs represent biases?
		Which strategies am I using to help monitor for bias?
		Did I use at least one strategy to monitor for bias during each phase of the research process?

planning and conducting a qualitative study should ask themselves. Being able to answer most of the questions as you create a research proposal will help you design a strong study. In fact, demonstrating trustworthiness is the primary method by which the strength of a particular qualitative study can be determined.

It is important to remember that no study is perfect. Accordingly, you will not be able to design a study that demonstrates high trustworthiness across each and every type. Instead, you can begin by picking about three or four strategies from those described in Table 10.2. This table also

Table 10.2

Strategies to Establish Trustworthiness

Strategy[a]	Description	Main type of trustworthiness enhanced	Information to report
Improve quality of general data collection	Have or obtain training in the research skills used in the study and the ability to establish a researcher–participant relationship	General	Training of those collecting or transcribing data, materials used, how rapport was established, anything done to help ensure participants were comfortable sharing the truth of their experiences
Increase intensity of general data collection	Spend enough time during data collection to ensure that you obtained enough information to answer your research question	General	Average and range of hours spent collecting data (e.g., interviews, focus groups), how much interaction occurred, average and range of transcript length
Widen access during data collection	Ensure that you were provided access to all relevant aspects of the lives, experiences, and culture of participants and the topic being studied	General	Amount and types of access
Adhere to ethics principles	Ensure that your research is ethical and participants are protected from harm	General	Institutional review board approval, how informed consent was gained, use of pseudonyms
Use rigorous research methods	Select methods based on those confirmed as rigorous	Credibility	Use of methodological citations and rationale for all methodological choices

Table 10.2

Strategies to Establish Trustworthiness (*Continued*)

Strategy[a]	Description	Main type of trustworthiness enhanced	Information to report
Engage in reflexivity	Spend time doing critical self-reflection of who you are and your biases, beliefs, and values. Engage in self-reflection in relation to the topic being studied, and spend time considering how your life experiences influence how you will hear or see and interpret those of participants	Credibility	Report that reflexivity took place without much further description or, preferably, a section (typically, a couple of paragraphs) added to the proposal or manuscript that shares these experiences with readers
Conduct negative case analysis	Actively seek a participant whose experiences do not fit with identified patterns or themes for the purpose of demonstrating multiple realities and accurately reflecting the experiences of the entire sample	Credibility	Report on your use of this strategy and description of the negative case analysis outcomes in the Results section
Use member checking	Reengage participants after data collection to help ensure that you are accurately reporting their experiences and to double check parts of transcripts	Credibility	Number of participants you asked for their thoughts about the findings, number who agreed with the findings, and any changes as a result of member feedback
Triangulate	Use multiple methods of data collection, multiple coders of data, and multiple theories for interpretation of data	Credibility	How triangulation was done and extent of consistency across multiple methods, coders, or theories

(continues)

Table 10.2

Strategies to Establish Trustworthiness (*Continued*)

Strategy[a]	Description	Main type of trustworthiness enhanced	Information to report
Use thick, rich description	Use rich and representative quotes when reporting findings	Credibility	Quotes that do a good job capturing a theme for a code
Gather background information	Provide enough description of the context or phenomenon of interest so others can determine whether the findings might apply to other people or situations	Transferability	Report on background from a literature review (what is known about the phenomenon) and description of methods (contexts and sample).
Maximize density	Describe the research process explicitly and with rich information	Dependability	Method description that is detailed enough for someone else to do the same study (replicability)
Use multiple coders	Use multiple coders to assess agreement on findings among them (i.e., the extent to which they would code the same thing in the same way)	Dependability	Percent agreement, intraclass correlations, kappa (interrater reliability statistic), and description of how disagreements were handled and how often coders met to discuss coding
Solicit an outsider perspective	Obtain the perspective of a coder not directly involved in the data collection or project	Dependability	Percentage of transcripts coded by the outsider using the established coding scheme, agreement with other coders, and procedures for handling disagreements.
Maintain an audit trail	Provide a complete accounting of every part of the research process, including all decisions made and how they were made	Confirmability	Description of audit trail and how it was used during the coding process

Table 10.2
Strategies to Establish Trustworthiness (*Continued*)

Strategy[a]	Description	Main type of trustworthiness enhanced	Information to report
Use journaling	Keep a journal during the entire research process and write about your reactions (e.g., emotional, psychological) during data collection or coding as a way to monitor for bias during the process	Confirmability	Description of how the journal was kept and used during coding
Use memos	Use memos to write down thoughts, insights, or potential codes during the analysis process	Confirmability	Description of how memos were used to track how themes emerged from the data

[a]Not all strategies are relevant for all qualitative designs. Some strategies strengthen multiple types of trustworthiness; we list only the main one or two types strengthened.

provides information that you should report in a proposal or manuscript when using a particular strategy in your project.

APPLYING CONCEPTS TO YOUR RESEARCH PROPOSAL

So, how do you pick strategies for your project? First, find similar research and see what the authors did. Second, consider the design of your study, and consider which strategies make the most sense. For example, let's suppose you decide to conduct a phenomenological study that focuses on understanding people's lived experiences. If that is the goal of the study, then you should select strategies that help you ensure you are accurately capturing the participants' experiences from their point of view. In this case, you can identify member checking as one strategy this fits really well with making sure you get it right.

Last, use the worksheet in Exhibit 10.1 to plan and justify your trust-worthiness strategy choices. This should help you think through and document the process (one way to actually demonstrate trustworthiness). Part of the worksheet is a column that asks you to identify a previous study that used the strategy you want to use (identifying more than one is great, too). Identifying strategies previously used is really important because (a) it demonstrates methodological rigor when you can cite a method that has been used before, (b) you can see how the authors incorporated the strategy into their project and use similar procedures for your study, and (c) it helps you understand why that strategy might be a good choice for you.

Now reread your proposal, especially the Design section, and add a section incorporating your plans for maximizing trustworthiness. Be sure to complete Exhibit 10.1 and include it.

Exhibit 10.1

Worksheet: Planning for Trustworthiness in My Study

Type of trustworthiness	Strategy	Rationale	Example citation	How they did it	My plans
Credibility	Member checking	This will ensure that I capture participants' actual lived experiences and do not misinterpret them.	Smith, 2016	They shared findings with 25% of their sample. When a participant disagreed, he or she was reinterviewed to gain a better understanding, and codes were altered to be more accurate. This process was reported in the Data Analysis section.	I will follow these procedures, except I will share findings with only 10% of my sample because I have only a semester to complete my project.

11

Conclusion

Congratulations! You have just designed your first research study and are ready to collect data and answer all of life's questions! Well, actually, the sign of a good research study is that it leads to more questions than it provides answers for. So don't expect too many answers, and when it is time to share your results with the universe, remember to end with a few new questions (i.e., future research) that you want to ask as a result of your findings. Aside from that, rather than write up some witty Conclusion chapter, we thought we would end with a few simple pieces of advice and reminders of some key points:

- Read a lot of background research and use theory, as well as your passion, to guide your study.
- Spend more time developing your study than it would actually take to collect and analyze data. In other words, it takes longer to plan and

http://dx.doi.org/10.1037/0000049-011
Designing and Proposing Your Research Project, by J. B. Urban and B. M. van Eeden-Moorefield

design a study than to conduct it. This is not something you can procrastinate on.

- Ask yourself whether you would let your closest family member or friend participate in your study. In other words, remember ethics!
- Pay attention to the little details—they are everything in research!
- Develop a flowchart that represents the experience of people participating in your study. Put yourself in their shoes to help ensure that the research process is clear and that you are protecting your participants. Again, ethics.
- Test everything out, and practice with friends.
- Work on designing your study in short chunks (i.e., don't try to do everything in one sitting, or even in a few sittings). Give yourself a lot of time.
- Make sure your proposal is internally consistent. The research questions and hypotheses should align with the sampling plan, design, measurement plan, and analysis plan.
- Remember, no study is perfect. Give yourself a break from any pressure you might feel to be perfect. Instead, plan thoughtfully and be aware of the limitations that are part of your study. As a bonus sure to impress, come up with a rationale for why a particular limitation was OK for your study, and have a citation ready to back it up.
- Speaking of citations, cite everything!
- Every research article you read is a resource and example—use them all to help out.
- Above all, have fun and embrace this journey. Maybe one day you will write a methods text of your own.

Good luck, and the warmest of wishes for success!

Index

About the Authors

Jennifer Brown Urban, PhD, is a professor in the Department of Family Science and Human Development at Montclair State University, where she also directs the Research on Evaluation and Developmental Systems Science lab. She is trained as a developmental scientist with specific expertise in youth development and program evaluation. Her scholarship is encapsulated under the umbrella of systems science, including both theoretical approaches and methodologies.

Dr. Urban's most recent research focuses on character development and innovative approaches to program evaluation and planning. She is currently principal investigator on several grant-funded projects. The goals of this work are to build the capacity of youth program practitioners and evaluators to engage in high-quality evaluation of character development programs, to determine the key features of character development programs that promote positive youth development, and to advance the application of character science in multiple contexts to enhance human flourishing across the lifespan. She uses mixed-method approaches in her own research and has mentored many undergraduate and graduate students in designing and executing applied research projects.

Bradley Matheus van Eeden-Moorefield, PhD, is an associate professor in the Department of Family Science and Human Development at Montclair State University and director of the PhD program. His research includes a strong social justice commitment to understanding and strengthening marginalized families, with his most recent work focused on stepfamilies headed by same-sex couples. Much of this research focuses on identifying how factors in the social world (e.g., stigma, stereotypes, policy) influence everyday family life and how each influence various indicators of individual (e.g., depression, happiness) and family well-being (stability).

Dr. van Eeden-Moorefield uses various qualitative and quantitative methodologies and has particular expertise in Internet-based methodologies. He has provided training to various family and child care practitioners and uses his previous clinical experiences to translate research into practice and practice into research.

About the Series Editor

Arthur M. Nezu, PhD, DHL, ABPP, is Distinguished University Professor of Psychology, professor of medicine, and professor of public health at Drexel University. In addition to currently serving as an associate editor of *American Psychologist,* he has held several previous editorial positions, including editor of the *Journal of Consulting and Clinical Psychology*, associate editor of *Archives of Scientific Psychology*, editor of *The Behavior Therapist*, and chair of the Council of Editors for the American Psychological Association. His research and program development in clinical psychology and behavioral medicine have been supported by the National Cancer Institute, the National Institute of Mental Health, the Department of Veterans Affairs, the Department of Defense, the U.S. Air Force, and the Pew Fund. Dr. Nezu has also served on numerous research review panels for the National Institutes of Health and was previous president of both the Association of Behavioral and Cognitive Therapies and the American Board of Behavioral and Cognitive Psychology.